B12

EARLY CHINESE
POTTERY AND PORCELAIN

The Faber Monographs on Pottery and Porcelain
Edited by W. B. HONEY

*

*

OTHER TITLES TO FOLLOW
Edited by ARTHUR LANE

White stoneware jar with impressed decoration. Ht. $13\frac{1}{16}$ *in.*
Shang-yin dynasty.
Courtesy of the Smithsonian Institution, Freer Gallery
of Art, Washington
See page 2

EARLY CHINESE
POTTERY AND PORCELAIN

by
BASIL GRAY

FABER AND FABER

24 Russell Square

London

First published in mcmliii
by Faber and Faber Limited
24 Russell Square London W.C. 1
Printed in Great Britain by
R. MacLehose and Company Limited
The University Press Glasgow
Blocks made by
Fine Art Engravers Limited Esher

Dedicated
to the members past and present
of the
Oriental Ceramic Society
through whose taste and knowledge
the study of early Chinese ceramics
has flourished
in London

FOREWORD

It is often asserted at the present time, that 'early Chinese pottery is the finest pottery ever made'; and it may well be granted that no other wares have shown a greater mastery of technique without ostentation, a finer sense of form and fitness in decoration, or a more discriminating sensuous appreciation of materials and glazes, than the Chinese wares believed to date from the ninth to the fourteenth centuries. They form a great repertory of masterpieces, and to choose enough specimens to fill the hundred plates in this book must have been a gratifying task. It is one which Mr. Basil Gray was particularly well qualified to perform. Succeeding that pioneer of Chinese ceramic studies, the late R. L. Hobson, Mr. Gray has charge of the oriental collections at the British Museum, and in addition to the learning required by that office, has the advantage of an eye trained by long study of Persian and Chinese painting. With this informed taste Mr. Gray has brought a new appreciation to bear on the great assemblage of Chinese wares in the British Museum, as well as in many private collections now again accessible after their banishment during the War.

W. B. H.

CONTENTS

ILLUSTRATIONS

COLOUR PLATES

MONOCHROME PLATES

PREFACE

Those of us who have in our keeping great collections of works of art are usually conscious of the obligation to show or publish them to the best advantage of all who appreciate them: we (probably) remind ourselves seldom of the privilege which we enjoy in handling and living with such things. This intimacy is something which can be shared to a slight extent with a wider public. Chinese pots were made to be touched and handled; as antiques they have lost, as well as gained something. They have acquired the finality which belongs to the work of another period, and of a different taste; but behind glass they are remote and insubstantial. Writing about such things is worth while if it sets them in focus historically or if it abolishes the show case and restores a direct relation.

This book forms part of a series, and it was decided that the earliest wares should be summarily discussed here and more fully treated in another volume on Primitive Pottery. At the Editor's express suggestion, although the volume covers the history of Chinese ceramics until the end of the Yüan period in 1368, no piece of blue and white porcelain is reproduced, and the story of the origins of this decorative style is left to be told in full in the volume devoted to the Ming period.

The illustrations are almost entirely taken from the rich resources in public and private hands in this country. I am indebted to all these owners for their kind permission to reproduce them and also for the freedom of access which they have allowed me to their cabinets. I am especially indebted to Sir Alan Barlow and Sir Harry Garner for entrusting to me the valuable vases from their collections while the colour blocks were being prepared, and to the latter for allowing me to use some of his analyses of glazes. The Director and Curator of the Percival David Foundation not only allowed me access to that wonderful storehouse before it was ready for opening, but at my suggestion welcomed a scientific examination of a Ting dish by the most searching tests.

The earlier literature of the period closed by the outbreak of the 1939 war was summed up in a convenient and masterly way by Mr. Honey in his *Ceramic Art of China* (1945) and he also surveys the Chinese sources for the history of ceramics in his Bibliography to this work (pp. 218–221).

The same ground is not gone over here but references are made to subsequent research and discovery.

In the choice of illustrations the accessibility of this and some other recent books has been taken into account and references to these have been made in the text to supplement the basis of discussion of the wares described. I owe a special debt to Mr. William Watson for reading the book in proof and for his pains in preparing the Index, and to Mr. W. Winkworth for much valuable advice.

B. G.
June 1952.

INTRODUCTION

In none of the higher civilisations of the world have ceramics held so prominent a place as in China, and nowhere has so sound a tradition of potting been built up. And so we find porcelain vessels or utensils ranking among the most precious possessions of the high official or scholar and treasured by emperors themselves.

Quality was preferred to intrinsic display of precious materials, or to profusion—not grand dinner services, nor gold plate are to be found, but perfection of form and glaze, vitality, elegance and appropriateness of decoration. Again, in no civilisation is it possible to see so clearly the value of a long tradition. The course studied and illustrated in this volume is of progress through generations of experiment to the superlative level of the Sung factories. The progress is a double one, on the one hand technical discoveries and improvements, and on the other the development of a sure and sensitive taste. Of course the progress cannot be summed up in the conclusion: for every age has its triumphs. But the kind of qualities found in Sung ceramics can come only as a result of many generations of appreciation of fine pots. And the basis was not a narrow one: there were countless kilns in different parts of China. The classic wares led the way but they were the leaders of a large company. The kiln sites are marked by large hills of wasters and seggars which testify to the scale of manufacture in these factories. In them definite types of wares and shapes were developed. No pot would have been unique in design, though each has the individuality of a handmade object. The standard was high and many pieces now treasured in the cabinets of collectors or the showcases of museums have survived because they were rejected at the time and thrown on one side.

None of the wares treated in this volume was marked with a factory name or even a period indication. A few individual pieces bear some kind of inscription but very few are beneath the glaze and therefore certainly original. One or two of these have been selected for illustration. But evidence of date and provenance has been slowly and painfully built up from finds both in and outside China, from literary references and from the tradition of later times. On Chinese soil there has been very little scientific excavation but this can be supplemented by excavations in Korea, Manchuria, Indo-China and Central Asia, and even as far afield as Mesopotamia and Egypt: surface finds have located a number of the main kiln sites but without themselves providing any evidence of date. For over fifty years Chinese texts have been searched for ceramic references, but the value of the evidence contained in them for the early period treated in this book is not great. Texts are only preserved in late forms in which bits have been redrafted or interpreted. Poetical references are too vague; the reports of foreigners too naive to tell us much.

CHINESE DYNASTIES

Shang-yin	1766–1122 B.C.
Chou dynasty	1122–249 B.C.
Han dynasty	206 B.C.–A.D. 220
The Six Dynasties	A.D. 220–A.D. 589
Sui dynasty	589–618
T'ang dynasty	618–906
The Five Dynasties	907–960
Northern Sung	960–1127
Southern Sung	1127–1279
Yüan dynasty	1260–1368

1

SHANG TO HAN DYNASTY

Prehistoric wares may be described as those which have not been associated with finds of inscribed material and to which only relative dates can consequently be given, in default of any extraneous references.

Attempts to establish a succession among these have been made by two Chinese scholars, the late Mr. G. D. Wu and Mr. Chêng tê-k'un, but these have not yet won full acceptance. The most notable types are the large mortuary urns discovered at several sites in Kansu and Honan. They are impressive in shape, with loop handles just below the full curve of the swelling sides. The decoration, in two or three colours, is well suited to the form and usually gives a turning movement either by sweeping spirals or by leaf-shaped diagonal strokes reserved in a black ground. Concentric circles and hatching are common, and some of the patterns, especially on urns from Ma ch'ang, in Kansu, seem to be undoubtedly symbolic, though of what one cannot be sure.

At some other sites however, principally in Shantung, and especially at Ch'êng-tzŭ-yai, another type of early pottery has been found, a finely potted black ware with burnished surface. Though it has not been found in association with bronze, this pottery has a definite connexion with the later bronze age. For it has been found sometimes associated with the divination bones treated in the same way as the well-known examples recovered from the Imperial bronze age site at Anyang in Honan; and in some of the vessels shapes are similar to the characteristic bronze vases and tripod cooking vessels of the Shang-yin period, the earliest known historic age of Chinese culture. However the black pottery is never found with inscribed material and it is at present very scarce and no whole piece has yet come to light.

Almost equally rare is a fine white ware found at present only at Anyang apart from a few fragments at Ch'êng-tzŭ-yai. So fine in texture is this ware that it has been taken for porcelain, but in fact the body is not of kaolin and it is to be regarded as a stoneware being made of carefully levigated clay fired at a temperature of about 1000° C. The decoration is clearly connected with that of the contemporary

B

1

bronzes, but conventionalisation of the motives is more pronounced—some, including claws, seem degenerate animals or birds while the only complete example known (1) is covered with chevrons all over the body. This type is contemporary with the Anyang site remains, about 1400–1100 B.C., and shows that good pottery was made in this period. It is clear that this fine white stoneware is nearly related to the 'bronze style'—the elements of decoration and the shapes of these vessels are indeed similar to that of the bronzes of the same period. So, it may be added, is the surface decoration of the marble carvings from the same site. But it has yet to be established that this style originated in bronze. It is perhaps more probable that it was evolved in pottery, and was then translated into bronze. It should be observed that the form of monster found on the white pottery is subordinated to the shape of the vessel in a way that the bronze decoration is not. An interesting pointer is that the Freer gallery vase shows a connection with the Pan-shan painted funeral pottery, closer than does any bronze vessel. It has also been pointed out that the decoration is carved into the surface of the vessel instead of being applied in relief and that the profile of the design is curved and not sharp-edged. Still it is not to be doubted that at the time bronze was the dominant material of craftsmanship.

This was to be true of much of Chinese pottery at least until the Han period. But some of the simple vessels are hand-thrown and decorated either with mats or with moulds applied to the surface. A pottery shape which seems to be derived from a metal original, but not a Chinese one, is the distinctive urn with wide-spreading handles springing from the lip made in a polished black ware and found in the stone tomb of the Lifan people in Szechwan.[1] Dr. Chêng tê-k'un has discussed the pottery of these people, who were in touch with Chinese culture but did not share in it, and has given reasons for dating these burials between 500 and 1 B.C. This seems a wide enough range, but it is considerably narrower than the extreme limits of date which had previously been suggested for this Lifan pottery.

Other late Chou wares from entirely Chinese areas include a few examples of the use of glass paste in decorating pottery. There is a covered bowl in the Kansas City Museum which was exhibited at the Royal Academy Exhibition of 1935–6, on which a rectangular design is carried out in glass paste, the crossings being further marked by segments of eye-beads applied as reliefs. This same technique of decoration is found on a bronze vessel from Chin-ts'un, and parts of beads are used to decorate some plaques of bronze. There is thus a fair

[1] Hobson *Handbook*, fig. 13.

(1) *Frontispiece*

presumption that the Kansas City bowl, and another very similar in the Sedgwick Collection (1), is of fourth–third century B.C. date. Dr. Sirén has remarked on the similarity of this applied decoration to that found on one of the bronze vessels, a *hu*, from Chin ts'un.

In this strange way was glaze first applied to the pottery body in China. On some earlier vessels (2) a gloss, which is in places glaze-like, has been caused by some accident during firing, such as wood ash falling on the heated pottery (cf. Hobson, *Handbook*, p. 4). But some glazed vessels have been attributed to the third century B.C. at latest. By that date finely potted hard fired vessels were being made (3). Some of them with characteristic bronze shapes are partly glazed (e.g. Hochstädter fig. 18) with a greenish or greyish glaze thinly applied and often perished. The range of shapes is limited to vases with tall necks, generously flaring at the lip, squat urns generally high-shouldered, and probably all originally provided with lids, and rarer specimens of tall amphorae. Nearly all are provided with loop handles often rather broad and of bronze form, and decoration is confined to them, to a combed wave pattern on the neck or shoulder, and to simple horizontal ribbing which greatly improves their appearance (4). The earliest securely dated piece is a vase from a tomb at Hsinyang, Honan dated A.D. 98.[1] Some were discovered by the Swedish railway engineer, Mr O. M. Karlbeck,[2] at Shouchou in Anhui whence similar bronzes have also come. In character of glaze and decoration these resemble a better-known class of ware to which the late Dr. Laufer gave the name 'proto-porcelain', having a purplish brown surface where the glaze has covered the red slip which appears below. It is known however that ware of this type was being used some two hundred years later, for a piece was found in a tomb of A.D. 299[3] and several in tombs at Pei-cha-ch'ing near Kalgan which are also dateable in this period.[4] And it is to the third century A.D. that the greater number of vessels showing this characteristic treatment have been ascribed.

The wares of the preceding Han period (206 B.C. to A.D. 220) are well known and easily described. They are of similar shapes whether glazed or not. The unglazed pots were, in all probability, intended to furnish the tombs with handsome-looking objects and are sometimes painted with swirling cloud motives, occasionally accompanied by animals which probably belong to another world than this. Sketchily painted figures also appear on these painted wares, generally of Taoist

[1] Hochstädter, fig. 20 and p. 106.   [2] *O.C.S. Transactions*, 1949–50, p. 33.
[3] Hobson in *O.C.S. Transactions*, 1934–5, p. 34 and pl. 6 (i).
[4] Pei-wei cf. *Archaeologia Orientalis* B, vol. V, 1946–7, fig. 16.

(1) *Plate* 1B; (2) *Plate* 1A; (3) *Plate* 5; (4) *Plate* 9.

inspiration (1). The style probably only reached full development after the end of the Han period, in such examples as the covered urn from the Eumorfopoulos collection in the British Museum, where the whole surface is covered with bands of carefully painted decoration in red and green. But the most characteristic pottery of the Han period is the green and yellow lead-glazed ware of decidely bronze shapes, often with moulded decoration (2). It is many years since any student of the subject doubted the true date of these wares, but even so, it is useful to have a dateable series like the pottery from the tomb of A.D. 98 at Hsinyang in Honan which was excavated by the Historical Museum of Peking.

In tombs in Manchuria, excavated by the Japanese, only unglazed pottery has been found; but in Korea where pottery is less plentiful in the tombs some glazed pieces are found: and it is rather more plentiful in the second century A.D. Chinese tombs of Annam excavated by the French Far Eastern School near Than-hoa. But all the pottery is wheel made whether it is glazed or not, and the shapes are decisive and satisfactory, if not of special beauty.

Once again it is principally pottery from the tombs that has come down to us, urns, watch-dogs, furniture and such things. Sometimes the vessels in green lead-glaze are clearly cheap substitutes for bronze (3). Although full of interest as social documents these wares generally have little aesthetic merit. Occasionally they reach a better standard and resemble the proto-porcelain or early Yüeh vessels (4), but usually such charm as they possess is from the iridescence of the glazes, decayed through long burial.

Although the surviving wares of the Han dynasty probably all come from tombs by excavation or chance finds, it is reasonable to suppose that vessels similar to the better quality pieces were used for domestic purposes. But the porcellanous Yüeh ware must have been preferred by all who could afford it. Pelliot has given reasons for dating the use of the character *tz'ŭ* to mean porcelain to the third century A.D. It does not occur in the original (Han) edition of the Shou-wen, but a chance mention by Pan Yo (A.D. 2–300) refers to central or eastern China and this may imply an earlier use in more metropolitan districts. Karlbeck has gone further in proposing a pre-Han date for the earliest type of wares with a 'celadon' or greyish-green glaze. A kiln site where this type was made was visited in 1937 by the late A. D. Brankston who obtained specimens which show the characteristic concave base. This site is called Nine Rocks (Chiu-yen) near Shao-hsing in Chekiang. The old name of Shao-hsing was Yüeh-chou and it is by this name that this general type is known. Brankston

---

(1) *Plate* 3; (2) *Plate* 4; (3) *Plate* 5; (4) *Plate* 6.

did not consider that any of the pieces which he obtained at Chiu-yen was earlier than the first century A.D. while others he considered as late as the sixth. Mr. Karlbeck[1] would, however, put the earlier types from Chiu-yen as far back as the third century B.C. on account of their resemblance, in style of decoration, to late Chou bronzes. It seems more likely that this olive-green glaze was made to imitate patinated bronze rather than, as is sometimes suggested, jade. Shapes certainly are traditional bronze types, such as *Ting* or *Ho:* but the decoration, which is apparently applied by using stamps to impress the clay before firing, seems more akin to the simple patterns of South China pottery[2] rather than to the complex designs of late Chou bronzes (1).

Among the bronze style features found in the early Yüeh-ware of Shao-hsing are bird spouts fully in the round; square loop-handles; wing-handles; monster-masks, generally only simulating ring attachments (2). All are covered with yellowish-olive or a brownish-green glaze, and the body is buff. A characteristic of this class of Yüeh ware is the slightly concave base found in all cases. The ware is much harder than in the ordinary lead-glazed vessels and the glaze is felspathic. At present, in default of excavated examples, it seems wiser to call this class 'Han or later'. On the other hand it is not difficult to find the stylistic connection of a noble vase with applied decoration, of tongue-panels and pearl pendants, and five developed *palmettes* round the neck (3). For these are characteristic of Sasanian Persia (224–642). It is consequently to be attributed to some kiln in the Six Dynasties period (A.D. 220–580). This is however a grey-bodied ware and the foot rim is flat and broad, and sharply cut, like the T'ang feet. Nevertheless the form and decoration of this monumental vase will hardly allow of its being later in date than the fifth or sixth century, and it may well be earlier than this. The closest parallel is with an unglazed vase from Khotan in the Berlin Museum collection with similar big handles and applied decoration (*Survey of Persian Art*, pl. 186b.).

A number of simpler Yüeh-yao vessels are unmistakably Han in date, for they reproduce typical Han bronze forms and decoration; dishes incised with two fishes, dippers, cooking-stoves, lobed wine cups like the well-known lacquered cups found in the Lolang tombs and elsewhere.

No pottery attributed to a later date than the sixth century was found at Chiu-yen, but not far away a second pottery kiln site near Shang-lin-hu, some thirty miles towards the sea has been located. This is discussed below (p. 16).

[1] *Oriental Art*, II (i), 1949.
[2] *E.g.* pottery found in the neighbourhood of Hong Kong by Fr. Finn and W. Weinberger, a good series of which is in the British Museum.

(1) *Plate* 7; (2) *Plate* 12; (3) *Plate* 13.

2

SIX DYNASTIES

If the Yüeh-yao and proto-porcelain types already discussed certainly extended from Han into the third century, there remains a gap without well-authenticated material in the period immediately following. Only from the Sui dynasty (581–618) is there once again reliably dated material in the furnishing of the tomb of Pu Jen at Anyang, Honan, in which was a tablet giving the date of death as A.D. 603. They consist of olive-glazed urns and bowls.[1] The urns have a distinct waist mark of a ridge at which most of the glaze stops short, and folded double loop handles. There are urns of a similar shape but more careful and sophisticated finish in the Victoria and Albert (Honey, pl. 11b) and the British Museum. Other examples, all from Loyang assigned to the Sui period by analogy are reproduced by Hochstädter (figs. 28, 30, 37 and 38). A still more finished vase, the well known white porcellanous four-handled piece in the Sedgwick Collection (Honey, pl. 30) is strikingly similar in general shape and in the form of the folded handles. This too may well be pre-T'ang.

A similar date has been proposed for the beginning of the extensive series of pilgrim-flasks with moulded decoration on the sides under a green or yellow glaze, on the ground of the simple technique and the softness of the ware. The pilgrim-flask shape is of course well known in early Christian sites of the near East and also in Parthia; but the form which is alone found in China, with flat foot, does not occur in Persia or Syria and is a Chinese modification. It must be admitted that the kind of late Hellenistic art reflected in the decoration of them is less likely to have been transmitted to China after the fall of the Sasanian empire at the Arab conquest in 642. The closest parallel for these subjects is found in some silver bowls in the British Museum and the Hermitage at Leningrad, but unfortunately the date of these is still unsettled. They are however in any case not later than the seventh century A.D.

It is with the ornament used in the famous hunting relief cut in the rock at Taq-i-Bustan between A.D. 610 and 626 that the closest parallel is to be found for the decoration of a very handsome type of

[1] Sirén, *3,000 Years*, vol. I, p. 432, figs. 317 and 318 and p. 439, fig. 328.

Yüeh vase, represented in the Ingram Collection (1) and the Kansas City Museum. It is true that the individual elements, rosettes, palmettes and strapwork, are equally appropriate to the early Sasanian period (third or fourth centuries). But the exuberant development of each feature and their multiplication is characteristic of the sixth to seventh century A.D. Whatever its precise date, this amphora is a striking example of western influence in Chinese ceramics, of which further account is taken in the next chapter.

A green and yellow glazed ware was certainly made in the sixth century as witnesses a child's sarcophagus in the British Museum, obtained in Szechwan, and dated the first year of the Liang Emperor Ta T'ung (or A.D. 527). Had it not been for the date in relief under the glaze of the end panel, the good-quality coloured glazes and style of the scrolls which decorate the upper borders would have suggested a T'ang date. In fact style does not coincide exactly with dynasty, and it will be seen that several of the T'ang styles continued into the late tenth and eleventh centuries, and of the Southern Sung styles into the Yüan and Ming dynasties. This is only a normal development.

Much the largest amount of tomb pottery from the Six Dynasties is, however, unglazed. These are the figures of attendants, musicians guardians and animals, once probably brightly coloured but now retaining only traces of red pigment (2).

---

(1) *Plate* 13; (2) *Plate* 24.

3

T'ANG

T'ang ceramics are weighty and monumental, and their most characteristic qualities of colour and form are handsome and impressive. The colour takes the eye, and the plastic form is vigorous and strong. For the first time effect was a primary consideration, and many T'ang vessels and stands seem to have been of little practical use.

It must, however, be remembered that the greater part of T'ang ceramics which have survived to our day are grave wares; either, like the figures, of types only serviceable for this purpose, or utensils made in showy imitation of the gold and silver plate of the contemporary fashion. We have long known something of the profusion of plate used by the Sasanians in Persia and by the Turks of Central Asia in the time of Menander (*c.* A.D. 568). Now we are beginning to have a better idea of its wide use in T'ang China, and we can appreciate how the various techniques of embossing and engraving silver came to influence the decoration of T'ang pottery.

This influence is perhaps most evident in the white wares of North China, for in them the whole shape of the silver vessel is often directly copied, and the elegant foliate forms, the serrated lips and splayed feet (1) all display typical metal lines. Chinese silver, if it was further decorated, was usually parcel gilt, and engraved. On the pottery, engraving under the glaze is not common on T'ang ware, except in the Yüeh type to be discussed later. But more elaborate ornament was frequently produced by the use of moulds which were pressed into the soft clay. These were most effective on a flat surface and the most handsome examples are the dishes in which the central feature is often a stylised lotus flower, or a complex of lotus flowers surrounding a bird in flight (2). These are picked out with coloured glazes, among which the chalky blue is the most beautiful, and the background sometimes variegated with a mottled or speckled glaze, contained by the incised ditches of the design (3).

It is noteworthy that the lotus so frequently figures in these designs, for it was imported to China from India by the Buddhist apostles and pilgrims in the early centuries A.D. Indian silver-plate is hardly known

---

(1) Cf. *Plate* 22A; (2) *Colour Plate* A; (3) *Plate* 32.

A. *Dish on three feet decorated with coloured glazes. T'ang dynasty.*
Diameter 11·3 in. British Museum
See page 8

to us, but there are indications that there may have been a large production, engraved after the style of the ivory panels found at Begram in Afghanistan by Hackin and his colleagues of the French Archaeological Mission. The sacred goose or *hamsa* and the lotus would have been prominent in any such products, this should not be forgotten when mentioning the well-documented influence in the decoration, both in design and technique, of T'ang pottery from the famous silver plate of the Sasanian period in Persia (A.D. 226–651). Sasanian art in general, and perhaps especially Sasanian silver-plate, may be regarded as the last representative of the art of the ancient world. Looking at it we can perceive a chain reaching back through Parthian and East Roman art to the earlier arts of the eastern Mediterranean— Greek, Scythian and Achaemenid. The motives which appear in so many materials preserve the clarity of their original conception in the glyptic art in marble, hardstone or gem. Both the vegetable, and especially the palmette, and the animal elements, generally fantastically combined in mythical creatures, remain monumental as they appear on these silver ewers and dishes. It is these elements, more than the pictorial hunting scenes, which fascinated the men of T'ang and appear on their coloured glazed pottery. In this connection is it worth noting in passing that Chinese silverware of this period, although showing Sasanian influence in the shapes, does not employ these large and bold Sasanian motives in its decoration. Much of the pottery buried with the dead in the T'ang period imitates both shape and decoration of Sasanian silver, especially ewers and vases (Honey, plates 18c, 20, 21), whose firmly splayed feet, ribbed necks and arched handles clearly reveal their origin. It is often stated that the spouts in the form of birds of prey which adorn the T'ang ewers are also derived from Sasanian prototypes, but this relation is not direct. The Sasanian silver ewers always show well-developed and firmly formed spouts, but these are never of bird form. On the other hand the bronze aquamaniles of the early Islamic period in Persia (eighth to ninth century) are regularly of bird or animal form with the head forming the spout; and the special emphasis on the head is found in the Sasanian period as a favourite motive in woven textiles. There is therefore little doubt that the bird's head spout in T'ang pottery does show Sasanian influence, but its use in this place should recall to us the long previous history of this bird spout in China, reaching back through the early Yüeh-yao pottery to the late Chou ritual bronze vessels.

No clearer evidence can be found of the mature character of T'ang art than its ability to borrow and adapt these western art forms and to produce from them such unified and satisfactory shapes as the typical T'ang ewer or vase, decorated with applied or moulded ornament under a white slip and splashed with coloured glazes—producing a very handsome appearance (1). Other T'ang pottery forms of western origin probably derive directly from the Mediterranean without Sasanian intermediary. Among these the most notable is the amphora—the Chinese form resembles the Hellenic prototype closely, except that the handles are usually dragon-formed and rise well above the lip of the vessel. Although vases of amphora shape with coloured glazes are not rare, the usual type is covered with a white glaze; an example in the Fogg Museum[1] is porcellanous, but its modified shape suggests a rather late date. The rhyton,[2] in spite of its Greek name, is an old Persian shape and its decoration as will be seen is of Middle Eastern origin. Before leaving the T'ang wares with western forms, mention must be made of the magnificent porcellanous ewer with eagle head below the lip which formerly adorned the Eumorfopoulos Collection and is now one of the great treasures of the British Museum.[3] This form when analysed is seen to be unusual. There was once a spout on its shoulder, no doubt short and straight as in the impoverished versions in Ting ware, as for instance one found in a Korean tomb of the Koryu period. We now know this Eumorfopoulos ewer to be a superb example of the Yung-ho kiln near Ching-tê-chên (in central Kiangsi, the Chi-chou of the Chinese texts).[4] The site, which will be mentioned again in connection with southern Ting-yao, was visited by A. D. Brankston in 1937.[5] He brought back fragments of the same hard ware, carved beneath the faintly yellow-green glaze. The ewer excels in both form and material; the neck is rather short, yet the strongly marked fourfold ridges in it strengthen it so that it is important enough to carry up the generous line of the body to the sculptural head. The fluent and graceful floral scrolls round the body and the elegantly flared mouth add the elegance of Sung to the strength of T'ang which meet in this, surely transitional, piece. A similar eagle head is found, this time as a true spout, on a typical T'ang ewer in Sasanian style,[6] thus showing its origin: but this Yung-ho ware is probably very late T'ang or Five dynasties, and the tenth century is the most likely date on stylistic grounds, as it will be shown to be also for the Yüeh ware of greatest distinction.

[1] O. Sirén: *3,000 Years*, II, p. 195, fig. 222.

[2] e.g. the Sedgwick cup reproduced Commemorative Catalogue, pl. 112, no. 983.

[3] Ashton and Gray, pl. 57; the colour plate in the Burlington Fine Arts Club catalogue of 1911 is much too green in tone.

[4] The Ko Ku Yao-lun states that pottery was still made at Chi-chou in the Yüan and Ming dynasties.

[5] *British Museum Quarterly*, XIII, p. 46.　　　　　[6] Honey, pl. 20.

(1) *Plate* 30.

Most distinctive of all the western shapes in common use in the T'ang dynasty is still the pilgrim bottle,[1] which may well deserve this name through having been brought to China by the early Buddhist pilgrims. Made by luting together two moulded roundels so as to form a flat vessel and adding a neck and two loop handles on the shoulders, this water vessel is one of the commonest utility shapes of blue glazed ware of the Parthian period in Persia. In the Sasanian period which followed it remained equally common, but was greatly reduced in size and is often found in burials in a purely symbolic state, with the side-walls so close to one another as to leave scarcely any space inside. In Syria however, both before and after the Arab conquest the pilgrim flask receives more decorative treatment and it is from the moulded design on these that the Chinese seem to have derived the brown and green glazed flasks which were in use before the beginning of the T'ang dynasty. Apart from a few Sasanian style ewers which show the same moulded type of ornament this is the only T'ang type on which human figures occur. The dancers, musicians, vintaging boys, or hunters on horseback seem to be rather of Central Asian than of Persian or Mediterranean type and costume, and they form a last and most distant echo of the half Hellenized art of Bactria. The animal on Mrs. Sedgwick's rhyton mentioned above resembles a Persian *senmurv* or lion-headed bird[2] rather than a Greek original of the Mediterranean.

Before leaving the T'ang wares in which foreign ideas have been used and adapted, a specifically Buddhist group should be mentioned. These are probably mostly made for burning incense though they are seldom complete (1). They should have a high foot and a pierced cover, the whole in metal form. On the sides are lion masks or Buddhist figures seated in meditation or as Bodhisattva enthroned, as on the rhyton in Mrs Sedgwick's collection.

In the year A.D. 851 there was produced, probably at Basra, an Arabic account of the East under the title *Ahbar as-sīn wa l-hind*, literally 'The story of China and India'. The unknown composer of this account has used the information brought back by several travellers, sailors or merchants among whom a certain Suliman was probably his principal source for his remarks about the colony of Moslem traders then established at Canton. His is the first Western mention of Chinese porcelain: which witnesses the reputation which the material gained at so early a date in so remote a centre. He writes of the Cantonese: 'they have pottery of excellent quality, of which bowls are made as

[1] Cf. p. 6.

[2] Cf. Smirnov, *Argenterie Orientale*, pl. LXVIV No. 132; and pl. CXXIII No. 307.

(1) *Plate* 23.

fine as glass drinking cups: the sparkle of water can be seen through it, although it is pottery.'[1] He was thinking of the well-known glass goblets of Syria when he made his comparison. The passage can be matched by one from a Chinese book, the Canons of Tea (*Ch'a Ching*) attributed to the poet Lu Yü who lived in the second half of the ninth century. He recommended as tea bowls the ware of Yüeh-chou, which were blue green (*ch'ing*) and lent a slight colour, comparable with ice and jade, to the tea; or of the ware of Hsing-chou which was as white as snow or silver. So early as this porcelain was esteemed for the two characteristics which have continued ever since to make its high reputation, the strength and reliability which permitted its export to remote countries, and its aesthetic qualities which gave it so high a place at home among the arts.

Modern accounts have tended to give so much greater prominence to the aesthetic side as to lose sight of the former. Nevertheless even in great modern collections, a large proportion of the Chinese porcelain is of a kind which was exported even if it was not made especially for the purpose. Both the white ware of Hsing-chou and the green ware of Yüeh found a ready market in the Arab world of the time.

Both types have been found on the site of the Abbasid palace city, Samarra on the Tigris, which was the summer residence of the caliphs during the short period from A.D. 836 to 883. Although it is certain that the great bulk of the material, excavated on this site by the German expedition under Sarre and Herzfeld before the first War, may be attributed to this period, it must be recognised that the site was not immediately deserted after the withdrawal of the court. This is proved by the existence of coins from the Samarra mint having dates as late as the year A.D. 1012. While therefore ninth century is no doubt the date of much of the imported Chinese ceramics found there, not all need be considered T'ang and the few fragments of Lung Ch'üan celadons may well be as late as the eleventh century. The most interesting of the Chinese export wares from the Samarra site is the white porcellanous ware, fragments of which have also been found in ninth to tenth century strata at Susa. It was so highly valued and rare after its long journey to Mesopotamia that it was imitated there by a local ware with a white slip beneath a colourless glaze.[2]

Is this porcellanous white ware the Hsing-yao mentioned in the *Ch'a-ching*? Modern ceramic scholars who have attempted to answer this question have generally cited pieces which resemble the fragments from Samarra. So it is best to start from a description of these. It is highly porcellanous, has a thick glaze, and the foot is cut roughly at the

[1] See the text and translation edited by Jean Sauvaget, 1950, p. 16, section 34.
[2] Cf. Arthur Lane: *Early Islamic Pottery*, 1949, p. 13.

edges. This is supposed to agree with the statement in the *Ch'a-ching* that the ware was 'used by rich and poor'. Sarre had long ago noted the correspondence of the Samarra fragments[1] with the descriptions of Hsing-yao, but only one of the pieces which he reproduces has the thickening of the rim which has been cited by Mr. Lindberg[2] as a mark of the ware, and none of those fragments from Samarra in the British Museum has this characteristic. The foliate shape which seems to be characteristic of T'ang white porcelain is also not represented at Samarra but it is found in the Mesopotamian imitations of the ware. Mr. Lindberg reproduces several examples of the T'ang white porcellanous wares in Swedish collections and Dr. Walter Hochstädter has published two bowls in the Buffalo Museum.

Mr. Koyama has called attention to a phoenix-headed ewer with iron-spot eyes preserved in Japan and all these are claimed as products of Hsing-yao. They may indeed be accepted as of T'ang or Five Dynasties date, but until the kiln-site of Hsing-chou in Chihli has been discovered it is rash to go further than to name the ware 'T'ang white porcelain'. In fact there seems a considerable range of white porcellanous wares of T'ang date. A bowl in the British Museum (1), which has a slightly thickened rim, is stated to have come from Tang Yang-Yu in Northern Honan. Another piece from the Raphael Collection (2) comes from a site '60 miles north of Kai-fēng fu' but may confidently be claimed as T'ang. A third bowl recently acquired by the British Museum is said to have been excavated at *Ch'ang-sha* in Hunan, south of the Yangtze, yet it closely resembles the first.

Other types of T'ang pottery which were exported to the West and imitated there by the local kilns include the dappled and splashed wares, green and orange, or manganese red. The finer wares of this kind seem also to have been admired in Japan, for in the Imperial Treasury of the Shōsō-in at Nara among the exquisite work in inlay and lacquer were dishes and bowls of this kind, and no other pottery except a vase and a porcellanous drumbody. Examples decorated in this way have been found in the tombs in China, but mostly smaller pieces, round boxes, saucers, and stands in which blue splashes are used mixed with the orange as well as green. Almost the only larger splashed pieces from the tombs are the covered storage jars on which rows of rosettes are left in reserve in the broad stripes of coloured glaze, but even these are comparatively small. Another type exported to the West as

[1] The best preserved are reproduced as plates XXV (1) and XXIV (2) of Sarre's *Die Keramik von Samarra*.

[2] Figure 5 in his article in *Ethnos* V.

(1) *Plate* 21; (2) *Plate* 22A.

well as found in burials in China is the marbled ware (1) made by mix-ing two differently coloured clays in the body and glazing with a trans-parent though sometimes coloured glaze. The general effect though not the technique of this marbled ware was imitated in the Moham-medan world.

The Yüeh ware, given the first place in the Ch'a-ching, and de-scribed as green (*ch'ing*) and like ice, is now identified by the discovery of the kiln site[1] in Yü-yao hsien in Chekiang, near Shanglin-hu where it was made both under the T'ang dynasty and later. It has a greeny-grey glaze over a grey porcellanous body. Under the foot are traces of piles of clay on which it was placed before firing in the kiln. It seems to have specialised in shapes of bowls and vases, and to have been usually decorated with engraved motives which at the best are both fine and accomplished (2, 3).

Fragments of Yüeh ware have been found in the rubbish heaps of Old Cairo (Fostât) as well as some at Samarra and Susa when it occurs in the tenth century stratum, but it was probably scarce there and highly prized. It seems likely that this type was widely used in China of that day for the ordinary occasions of life, and was imitated at many local kilns. Decoration and shapes are entirely in Chinese taste. From it one can obtain a good idea of T'ang taste in pottery: it is more elegant and sophisticated than the tomb pottery; unlike most T'ang wares it has a foot-rim, usually splayed outwards (4). Some of the engraved decoration is beautifully free. This is the scholar's ware and typical of T'ang official and literary society: but the main current of the age is better represented by the richly coloured wares with their echoes of distant trade with the West. Political intrigue might give rise to escapism, but the mood of expansionism—confident and strong—was the dominant one of the age.

That the T'ang style did not cease abruptly with the fall of the dynasty is clear. A good deal of archaeological surveying has been carried out by the Japanese in Manchuria. The area of Jehol was occupied from A.D. 907 to 1124 by the Liao people, who enjoyed a civilisation to all intents and purposes Chinese. Among the ceramic finds, now preserved in the Mukden Museum, are not only typical Northern Sung wares, Ting, Chün, Tz'ŭ-chou and Celadons, but also three-colour and yellow and green glazed monochromes over a white slip, wares completely in the T'ang tradition. Two covered boxes in the Mukden Museum in three-coloured glazes, but rather more advanced in style, have been published in a Japanese periodical

[1] See Y. Matsumura, Exploration of Yüehchou kiln sites in *Toji*, VIII, 5, 1936.

---

(1) *Plate* 33; (2) *Plate* 14; (3) *Plate* 15B; (4) *Plate* 15A.

(*Oriental Ceramics*, XII, 4). On one is incised a hare, on the other a freely drawn flower. Decoration of this kind is unknown on the T'ang three-coloured vases.

The T'ang date of a famous series of large pottery figures of the Lohan of which the finest is in the British Museum has, from the time of their discovery in 1910, been questioned by some scholars, and most recently by Dr. Reidemeister, who in an important article (Ostasiatische Zeitschrift, N.F. 13, 1937) sought to identify the harder body and brighter glaze with some of the pottery found on the Liao sites in Manchuria. He admits, however, that some shards of this type were found at Samarra; and the contrast he makes with this kind of ware is only decisive as against the T'ang grave pottery. He also brings forward again an argument first employed by his former chief in the Berlin Museum, Dr. Kümmel, in 1914, namely that the cult of Lohan in China was only fully developed in the eleventh century. This is undoubtedly an exaggeration. This cult was introduced from India in the fifth century, and given an impetus by the Buddhist pilgrim Hsüan-tsang in the seventh; and employed a specialist painter Kuan-hsiu in the ninth. This tradition is known to us from Lohan paintings of the tenth century at Tun-huang (Pelliot, *Grottes, III*, pls. 150–151). Images in the round may be a later development than paintings of Lohans, but there is a record of the casting of a set of eighteen in 959 in a sanctuary in Kwangsi, (cf. S. Lévi, Les Seize Arhats protecteurs de la loi, *Journal Asiatique*, XIe série, Tome VIII, 1916, pp. 269–70, 273, 276 and 287).

The final argument which Dr. Reidemeister adduces is stylistic. He cites for comparison the twelfth century wooden figures of Shansi, and those of the Kamakura school in Japan which derive from them. In this he seems to be on surer ground: but an even closer parallel in style can be found in some dry-lacquer figures of the end of the eleventh century.[1] Among marble sculpture a headless Buddha, now in the Freer Gallery, Washington, may be cited for comparison. This is dated 1032 (cf. Sirén, *Chinese Sculpture*, pl. 417). There seems good reason to attribute this fine series of ceramic sculptures to a period no later than the eleventh century, and more probably to the ninth or tenth century, but it seems hardly likely that they were originally placed in the I-chou cave in Chihli in which they were found. It is indeed hardly likely that such remarkable achievements of the potters' craft could have been produced except in a metropolitan kiln. The Liao were in control of parts of Chihli and they might have been made at that time: but they are altogether superior in body and glaze to the wares found on the Manchurian sites.

[1] Cf. A pair of Lokapala of 1097 cited by Dr. Sirén, *3,000 Years*, II, pp. 128-9; and one in America dated 1099 reproduced in *University Prints*, pl. 203.

4

FIVE DYNASTIES

The early wares of Yüeh type have already been discussed and it has been pointed out that they are the earliest high-fired hard-paste products of the Chinese kilns, and therefore the ancestors of all the coloured porcelains. Important as are the Tê-ch'ing and Chiu-Yen kilns for this reason, the new kilns at Shang-lin lake were to have far greater fame and influence. For their products reached every part of China and were exported by sea to distant regions of the West. It found its way to Japan and fragments have been found at Samarra in Iraq, at Fostât in Egypt, and at Susa in southern Persia. The archaeological evidence provided by these finds would confirm a date for these wares covering the ninth to the early eleventh century. This agrees with the period of the princes of Wu and Yüeh who ruled at Hangchow from 907 to 976, for whom a private kiln is said in the *T'ao Shuo* to have made a precious reserved ware of jade-like green. Further indication of its colour is given by the report of Hsü Ching (A.D. 1124) on Korea, in which the local celadon, well-known to us from the finds in graves of the Koryu period, was said to resemble 'the old pi-sê (or private) ware of Yüeh-chou'—which also carries the suggestion that these kilns were then no longer active. Wasters and fragments from the Shang-lin-hu lake kiln site, near Ning-po, in Chekiang, were collected by Dr. M. Nakao in 1930 and some of these are in the British Museum study collection. The date of these is corroborated by two finds made in the foundations of Japanese temples, believed to have been built, one in A.D. 904–5, and the other in A.D. 1005.[1]

It is a grey-bodied ware, turning dark red when exposed in the kiln, and the foot generally shows a rather high splayed rim, inside which are often seen traces of the fire-clay rings on which the vessels rested during firing. With this evidence it has been possible to identify many examples now to be seen in the principal public collections of England and America. But the largest series is that assembled by Sir Herbert Ingram, and this has been drawn upon in the choice of illustrations in this volume (1). Decoration is usually carved or incised, and frequently

[1] See Koyama in *Artibus Asiae*, XIV, p. 37–8.

(1) *Plates* 12, 13, 17–20.

includes foliage or *palmettes* in panels and a combed leaf frieze round the body near the base. Lotus petals are often deeply incised on the outsides of bowls or water-pots, but sometimes the body is deeply carved either with foliage or more elaborate decoration. A particularly fine type of deep bowl on high foot rim has waves carved outside and two dragons pursuing a pearl inside. Examples of this kind are in the Metropolitan Museum, New York (Honey, pl. 32b,) and the Ingram Collection (1). A third bowl in the Percival David Foundation has the rim encased in gold, recalling a passage in the *T'ao Shuo* to which Hobson drew attention:[1] 'the gold band enhances the brilliance of the precious bowls'.

The transitional position of this ware between T'ang and Sung can be seen in the development of the shapes, particularly the tall covered vases, some of which still have mouths with sharply rectangular profiles and well marked necks, while others (2) show a further and smoother transition from neck to body, thus approaching a Sung shape.[2] Also in the Ingram Collection are some toilet-boxes, with moulded decoration, a technique which Hobson thought was never used in Yüeh-yao—they are probably of early Sung date. On the other hand a well-known type of saucer dish with a linear design of two phoenixes[3] has a thoroughly T'ang flavour. The colour of the glaze varies in this ware from a greyish to a bluish green, and it is usually rather thinly applied, but the foot is completely covered. It seems likely that the Ch'ai ware of Chêng-chou, so well-remembered in later times as another royal preserve, in this period, of the emperor Shih Tsung (945–9) but now unidentified, was a northern variant or imitation of Yüeh-yao, with blue-green glaze resembling the Koryu celadons. If so it may be considered a predecessor of Ju-yao, with a similar buff body, made in the neighbouring province of Honan. A very beautiful lobed bowl from the W. C. Alexander Collection, now in the British Museum,[4] conforms with the opinion held in the Ming and Ch'ing period of a ware more finely potted than the best Yüeh-yao and with dense and even blue-grey glaze. Although sadly damaged, this bowl has great quality and it cannot be classed with any of the established wares. It was regarded by Hobson as perhaps of Tung ware, but here for this ware a different identification is suggested.

[1] O.C.S. *Transactions*, 1936–7, p. 14–15.

[2] That the ware continued into the early Sung dynasty is proved by a fragment from Shang-Lin-hu, in the British Museum, dated, under the glaze on the base, A.D. 978.

[3] Ashton and Gray, pl. 73B: Honey, pl. 32A.

[4] Hobson *Handbook*, 1937 and 1948, fig. 40.

(1) *Plate* 17; (2) *Plate* 18.

5

NORTHERN SUNG WARES

In the Northern Sung period which ended with the flight of the emperor Hui Tsung before the Chin Tartars in A.D. 1127 from his capital Kai-fêng, the centre of Chinese civilisation was in the valley of the Yellow River; and the kilns of the northern provinces, Chihli, Shansi and Honan supplied the needs of the court. According to the almost contemporary evidence of the *Pi hêng* of Yeh Chih quoted in the *Chuo Kêng-lu* of 1368, the imperial factory was established near the capital in the Chêng-ho period (1111–1117) by the emperor Hui Tsung to produce a new 'official' (*Kuan*) ware to take the place of Ting-yao, hitherto the palace ware, on account of the defects in the glaze of the latter. It will therefore be assumed here that Ting-yao was the first imperial ware of the Sung period and it will be given the first place in this account of the Sung wares. But it should be stated in advance there were certainly important kilns existing at this time in the south, in the provinces of Fukien and Kiangsi, and also in Chekiang, the province which became the principal ceramic centre when the capital was transferred in the Southern Sung period to Hangchow.

Although the imperial kiln of Ting-chou has not at present been located in Chihli, the identification of Ting-yao is certain, for its characteristics of 'tear marks' in the creamy white glaze correspond with descriptions in early texts. As early as the sixth century the 'white porcelain of Ting-chou' is mentioned by T'ao Yin-chü.[1] But apparently in the time of the poet Su Tung-po (1036–1101) there was also a red Ting-yao like 'polished red jade'.

The *Ko-ku Yao-lun*,[2] followed by the *T'ao Lu*[3] also mention 'purple' and 'black' Ting. But the last reference may refer only to imitation Ting-yao made at Ch'ang-nan (i.e. Ching-tê chên), in which the white porcelain body is completely covered with black glaze. Of this kind are two bowls on ball feet now in the British and Bristol Museums.[4] These cannot be accepted as Sung pieces. 'Black' Ting of earlier date is best classed with the Northern Black Wares discussed

---

[1] Quoted by Friedrich Hirth, *Origins of Porcelain*, 1888.
[2] Quoted by A. L. Hetherington, O.C.S. *Transactions*, 1928–30, p. 28.
[3] Ed. Sayer, pp. 50–51.
[4] The Schiller Collection, pl. V, Bristol City Museum, 1948.

below. As Hobson remarked in his introduction to the David catalogue (p. xxx). 'The thick black glaze . . . was used in many parts of China . . . it appears on a different body, as for instance on the Tz'ŭ-Chou wares which are made of buff grey stone-ware and on those of Honan factories which have a white porcellanous body, albeit sometimes dressed with a wash of black clay'. To these should perhaps now be added the Chin Tz'ŭ T'sui-yao site discovered by Koyama in central Chihli,[1] but the few fragments of black glazed ware found on this site (examples of which are in the Percival David Foundation) may all be intrusive. In any case they differ in body from the Tz'ŭ-chou type. 'Purple Ting' on the other hand has been identified by some Japanese archaeologists with a Northern Brown glazed ware with a warm yellow-brown glaze tending sometimes toward an aubergine purple. This is not particularly common but examples are in most large collections, and it has been found in Korean tombs. It is well to state here, as will be made plain later, the border between the different Northern wares is not well defined so that Ting, Black glazed, and Tz'ŭ-chou types are found on the same sites and were perhaps made in the same kilns. It seems most convenient to confine the term Ting-yao to the finely potted faintly orange-bodied ware with a high-fired white glaze which appears brownish or greenish where it runs more thickly in streaks known to the Chinese expressively as 'tear-drops', which, according to the *Tsun Shêng Pa Chien* of Kao Lien (1591), characterised the best Ting pieces.[2] This is the course which has been followed here, and it permits the grouping of similar wares with white glaze, round a classic name, as 'Ting types'.

All the evidence points to Ting-yao being the ware in which many characteristic Northern Sung shapes were first developed. For instance, when Hsü Ching visited Korea in A.D. 1124 he observed that the native Koryu wares in general copied the forms of Ting-yao. There is a beautiful depressed globular ewer and deep basin, in which it is made to stand, of *Ying-ch'ing* ware which entered the British Museum with the Eumorfopoulos Collection,[3] which can be matched in shape by a Koryu celadon version found in a Korean tomb.[4] The explanation is that the prototype of both wares was of Ting-yao. A Ting ewer of a shape not far different is in a Japanese private collection.[5]

It has already been remarked that Ting-yao follows after a T'ang

[1] Toji XVII (2). Dec. 1941.

[2] *Year Book of Oriental Art*, I, 1925, p. 86.

[3] Catalogue, vol. VI, pl. XIX: cf. Charles B. Hoyt Collection, Memorial Exhibition, 1952, No. 380.

[4] Prince Li Museum, Vol. 1, fig. 255.

[5] *Kokka*, No. 707, Feb. 1951, pl. 7.

white ware, perhaps made in the same locality, which was porcellanous, but had not yet achieved the perfection of potting and smooth density of glaze of the Sung Ting. Since it is not possible to follow the transition from T'ang to Sung in dated or datable examples, it is worth while to notice where the Ting-yao shapes are clearly developed from shapes found in T'ang pottery. Among the T'ang three-coloured wares an admirable shape is the vase with ridged trumpet mouth and spreading solid foot.[1] A transitional shape is seen in a white vase with foliate mouth in Sir Herbert Ingram's collection (ibid, No. 43); and the Sung form fully developed in Ting-yao, Northern Black ware[2] and painted T'zŭ-chou wares. In the Percival David Foundation is a Ting dish[3] with chalky white glaze and broad foot-rim which has the rim strengthened by a thick flange, both of which features suggest an early date, not long after T'ang and most likely the tenth century. It bears a four-character mark inside the bowl under the glaze 'Ting-chou kung yung', or Ting-chou for general use, thus suggesting that a 'private' or imperial ware was already being produced at the Ting-chou kilns. In the same collection, which is so rich in inscribed pieces, is a finely potted Ting-yao foliate dish without foot-rim, with a single character 'Kuan' (official) incised under the glaze. It is unlikely that in Sung times this mark meant more than it said, that the piece in question was supplied to the palace. It is only at a much later date that *Kuan* became attached exclusively to a single type, namely the celadons made at the Hangchow Surveyor's Office (Hsiu-nei-ssŭ).[4] *Ting* was superseded by *Ju* as the palace ware. It became natural to speak of this as '*Kuan*', but no marked piece is in fact known. Whether this can legitimately be described as 'Kuan Chün', or if it is in fact no other than Northern Kuan (*Pei Kuan*), as has been suggested by Sir Percival David, such official wares accord well with Chinese practice and ideas at this time and indeed during many centuries of her history. But it is probably foreign to the practice of the Sung period that such official pieces should have been made only in a single factory, as was later the case with the imperial factory at Ching-tê-chên under the Ming and Ch'ing dynasties.

It is simplest, and therefore best, to allow a variety of types of Kuan-yao under the Sung and to suppose that they were made at a number of different kilns, employing different types of clay for the body, and with glaze varying in fusibility, density and colour, sometimes crackled and sometimes not. In general all these diverse types probably reflect differences of taste in the potter, who well knew

[1] Cf. O.C.S. T'ang Exhibition, 1949, No. 148 and plate from Mrs. Sedgwick's collection.

[2] Honey, pl. 54A.   [3] Hobson, *Catalogue*, pl. XCI.   [4] See below, p. 37.

how to control his materials and to regulate the conditions of firing so as to obtain the effect that he desired.

But to return to the Ting wares. The most characteristic Ting shape is a conical bowl on a small foot, but the most beautiful are the deep bowls with foliate rim. Both these types were fired upside down in the kiln, resting on their rims which are consequently bare of glaze and are usually afterwards protected by bronze sheaths. Large vessels, ewers or basins are often decorated with bolder designs carved in the body with a knife. Sometimes such a treatment of the outside is combined with a freely drawn incised design inside the vessel. Undecorated pieces were also made in large numbers and these often achieve great distinction of form (1). Many pieces have been recovered from the site at the city of Chü-lu-hsien near the borders of Chihli and Shansi, which was submerged A.D. 1108 by a change of course of the Yellow River. As a result of long burial in water-logged ground the glaze of these pieces has crazed in a way easily recognisable, and the surface has become dull like an ostrich-egg (2). But the finest white Ting-yao is not of this kind but has a more intense and denser glaze with an assured refinement of shape comparable with the other classic Sung wares, Ju and Kuan (3).

An important kiln site at which Ting type porcelain was at least the principal product was discovered in 1941 by Dr. Koyama at Chien-tz'ŭ-Ts'un in central Chihli. He has described[1] the innumerable fragments of white ware, and the masses of kiln waste, and reported that the carved and incised wares greatly outnumbered the moulded pieces which seem only to have amounted to about one per cent of the total. There was a great deal of plain white porcelain, and also fragments of red and black glazed ware already referred to. One technique noted here was the use of iron to form small spots of ferruginous brown decoration. This technique is occasionally seen on complete specimens in collections, as for instance a small box from Mr. Oppenheim's collection in the British Museum, and in the eyes of two rabbits on octagonal bases, (for use as paper weights) found at I-chou in Chihli, and now in the Percival David Foundation and the British Museum. A Ting ewer in Japan has a flower pattern in iron on the handle. At

---

[1] *Toji*, XVII (2). Dec. 1941; Bulletin of Eastern Art, Nov-Dec. 1941. Cf. J.M. Plumer in *Archives of Chinese Art Society of America*, III, 1948–9.

(1) *Plate* 37.

(2) *Plates* 38, 48, 50. Northern black ware, Tz'ŭ-chou and Ying ch'ing types have also been recovered from this site which of course confirms a Northern Sung date for them.

(3) *Plates* 39 and 42.

Chien Tz'ŭ-ts'un the evidence was that most pieces had been fired upside down in the kiln. Unfortunately the illustrations to Koyama's articles are either of pieces identified by comparison with the fragments or quite small fragments. It appears that stone-ware of Tz'ŭ-chou type was also made at this kiln; an idea which is supported by the account of the Ting-chou products given by Kao Lien in his somewhat unreliable *Tsun Shêng Pa Chien* of 1591, where painted Ting-yao is mentioned including figures of Lohans, Immortals and children, and coloured jars and vases five inches to two feet high. Evidently we should call what is here described as of Tz'ŭ-chou type, and the moral is that it is a mistake to draw too hard and fast a line between Ting types and Tz'ŭ-chou types. They were probably often made at the same kilns, and to some extent complement one another in shape and use.

It is recorded that when the court fled to the south in 1127 some of the potters from the Ting kilns emigrated too, and established fresh kilns in the district of Chi-Chou in Kiangsi.[1] These kilns were stated to have continued in operation till the Yüan and Ming dynasties. The evidence given above should make it quite clear that the Northern Ting ware is identified beyond any shadow of doubt and its early date fully established. Yet there is a persistent belief in China that the finest type of Ting-yao was made at Chi-Chou and consequently all the finest pieces are assigned to this kiln. The reason for this remained obscure until two marked pieces turned up, of which one, now in the Percival David Foundation, has become celebrated,[2] the other in the private collection of Mr. Kuo Pao-ch'ang is at present unpublished. Both mention Yung-ho, which is in Chi-an prefecture in Kiangsi, and the Shao-Hsing period (A.D. 1132–62), and both state that these dishes were made by the Shu family, who are mentioned in the passage in the *Ko-Ku-Yao-Lun* already referred to. Mr. Kuo's dish has an exact date equivalent to A.D. 1143. The dish in the Foundation has the mark in slip under the glaze in very neat characters. Although this mark is quite unlike any other on Sung wares, and its very complete-ness naturally gives rise to suspicion, a careful examination by micro-scope and sheen glossmeter reveals no difference in the glaze covering the base over the inscription from that on the rest of the dish. Yet the dish would be accepted by all students of the subject as of Ting-yao indistinguishable from the products of the Northern kiln. This then is presumably the explanation of the Chinese ascription of these to Chi-chou.

In 1937 Brankston[3] visited the Yung-ho village and obtained

---

[1] *Ko-Ku-Yao-Lun.*   [2] Hobson, in *Burlington Magazine*, Dec. 1935.
[3] O.C.S. *Transactions*, 1938.

wasters and pottery fragments from the kiln sites there. One fragment has already been referred to in connection with the identification of the Eumorfopoulos phoenix ewer. He states that the 'best known' of the wares from Yung-ho is an 'imitation of Ting-yao', with body varying from soft buff to a hard white or gray stone-ware, of which the white is almost porcelain. But unfortunately among the fragments which he brought back from Yung-ho and which are now in the British Museum there is no example of the type. There are brown glazed fragments with a hard white body. He stated that some of these also were marked 'Shu chian kung fu', that is, made by the Shu family, but none has so far been published. He describes the mounds of refuse to be seen on this kiln site, and it is to be hoped that further examination of it will be made. Meanwhile the existence of southern Ting must be accepted, but it is impossible to distinguish it from the products of the Chihli kilns. These probably also continued in the southern Sung period, but the evidence cited by Hobson of a dish found in a twelfth-century tomb in Manchuria in 1887 and now in the British Museum[1] is not conclusive, for this might have travelled and been highly regarded on that account. It has an incised design of good quality but the potting is not of the highest class. Two pieces of Ting ware bearing dates are reproduced here (I). The first of these which carries a date of 1162 in ink under the base is a covered jar of a shape near to the T'ang, but the cover is incised in true Sung taste. Probably this is a southern Sung piece and much of the moulded Ting is likely to be so too. A stem cup in Mrs. Clark's collection (2) is of a shape which can be exactly paralleled in Lung-chüan celadon[2] and certainly not earlier than the twelfth century, and perhaps as late as the thirteenth. The second dated piece, a dish incised with a fish and flowers, is from the beginning of the Yüan dynasty and this mark is incised in a true style similar to the design under the glaze on the reverse.

The second largest family of Northern kilns is grouped under the name of Tz'ŭ-chou, a district in South-Western Chihli near the border of Northern Honan, which is mentioned in the *Ko-Ku-Yao-Lun*. The district is still a centre of ceramic production and there must have been many kilns there in the Sung period. One of these was located by Dr. Koyama in 1942 at Tzŭ-hsia, Chihli[3] and more recently he has revisited one reported by Mr. Karlbeck as long ago as 1933[4] at Chiao-tso in Northern Honan near the Shansi border and also not far from Chihli and Tz'ŭ-chou. The ware, which is best described as

[1] Hobson, *Handbook*, fig. 49. [2] C. B. Hoyt collection, No. 227.
[3] *Bijutsu Kenkyu* No. 134, 1944. [4] *Ethnos*, vol. III, 1933.

(I) *Plates* 38 and 44B; (2) *Plate* 47A.

Tz'ŭ-chou type, is a stoneware much more heavily potted than Ting-yao, and mainly employed for vases, wine jars, brush pots and pillows. The buff body is covered with a white slip in preparation for decoration, painted, carved or incised. This slip often stops short some distance above the foot. Not only are the Tz'ŭ-chou vases worthy of a good deal of attention for their intrinsic qualities of form and decoration, but they have a particular significance in the history of Chinese ceramics as the first type painted under the glaze. The first pieces were probably made early in the Sung dynasty, in the tenth or early eleventh century, and it was soon established as the ware in greatest demand for everyday use among all who could afford it. The commonest style of decoration, and also the most effective, was a simple design of one or more sprays of foliage, bamboo or orchid, brushed calligraphically in black or brownish-black slip, and afterwards covered with a colourless glaze. Sometimes the slip is carved away and the design thus formed is then covered with a colourless or a coloured glaze. The most striking use of colour on these 'graffiato' wares is a green which appears very deep over the black slip, and less intense where it has been carved away. A vase of this kind from the Koechlin Collection is in the Musée Guimet, and a well-known large vase of exceptionally beautiful shape is in the British Museum (Eumorfopoulos Collection) (1). This technique lends itself to bold design especially on large objects like wine vessels, and pillows, one of which, in the British Museum, is dated A.D. 1071 (2). Even more beautiful than those, like this, carved through a brown slip, are those carved in a white, which contrasts after firing, with the greyish buff of the glazed body (3). The shape of this suggests an attribution to the Southern Sung period. This carved technique is less frequently employed than engraving or incising through the slip (4).

Now both the painted and graffiato techniques of decoration were known in the Near East from an earlier date. It seems likely therefore that the Islamic world thus repaid the debt it owed to China for the T'ang splashed wares and the white porcellanous wares. It may be that yet another kind of Tz'ŭ-chou decoration, painting in black under a turquoise glaze, may owe something to the Near East where this was a favourite style of decoration at least from the twelfth century. But here the evidence is still insufficient. It has been customary to attribute this style to the Yüan and early Ming periods, and certainly the shapes of the vases and the drawing of the pictures seem to go best with the type of blue and white which is attributed to the fourteenth century. But the Japanese have found examples both in Korean tombs of the Koryu period and also in the Liao country including a tomb in Manchuria

---

(1) *Colour Plate* B; (2) *Plate* 55B; (3) *Plate* 56; (4) *Plate* 53.

B. *Vase with green glaze over a black slip carved with peonies. Tz'ŭ-chou ware. Sung. H. 15·4 in. British Museum*
See pages 25, 28

where there was a sarcophagus with the date A.D. 1018. This last vase[1] is almost identical with several vases in Western collections including one from the Eumorfopoulos Collection in the British Museum (1). In lobed cartouches of Islamic shape, which are also seen on other Tz'ü-chou types, are hares and figures in landscapes. It is hard to admit so early a date as 1018 for this type and precise evidence on the undisturbed state of this tomb is required. Nevertheless it is perhaps probable that this type of painting was first introduced to China with the turquoise glaze and only later used at Ching-tê-chên on blue and white. The Islamic parallels would certainly allow of an early thirteenth-century date for these vases.[2]

Some use was made too at the Tz'ŭ-chou kilns of an even more advanced technique, enamelled decoration over the glaze. And this too probably goes back to the early thirteenth century at least and the more primitive pieces may be securely attributed to Sung. These shew a simple design of red flowers on a green ground sometimes with a yellow border. A small dish of this type, preserved in Japan,[3] bears on the base a date in ink 'Tai-ho 1st year', equivalent to A.D. 1201, and another example with the same colouring is in the Seligman Collection (2). The colours at this time were limited to tomato red, sage green, and a raw orange-yellow, and these were ill-controlled and are frequently degraded in surviving specimens. But such defects are compensated for by the freshness of invention and handling so often found in experimental work. Another piece in Japan bears a much earlier date and would suggest a manufacture in the Liao country. This is a large covered jar decorated in red, yellow, turquoise and purple-blue enamels with figures in landscape in panels, and is dated in red enamel on the side about half an inch from the base, 'Tenth year of Taipeng' equivalent to A.D. 1030. This was in the sale of the property of Kitaoji Rogo in 1934 but until the authenticity of the date can be vouched for by some competent investigator, it is difficult to accept so early a date for the technique, and best to class it with a beautiful vase in the Victoria and Albert Museum, Eumorfopoulos Collection,[4] decorated with hares and foliage with yellow bands and a brown enamel on the neck. This more advanced and better controlled technique probably dates from the fourteenth century at earliest. It is

[1] *Toji*, 1941. For shards of the type see R. Torii, *Culture of the Liao Dynasty* 1936, pl. 338.

[2] Cf. C. B. Hoyt Collection, Nos. 293–4.

[3] *Kokka*, No. 378, colour plate.

[4] Sirén, 3,000 Years, fig. 357; Eumorfopoulos Collection Catalogue vol. III pl. LVI.

(1) *Plate* 59; (2) *Plate* 58.

of great interest as the first example of a technique so widely developed in the Ming dynasty and later. The simple enamelled pieces are not uncommon, and they have been found in Korean tombs[1] but the only piece with a Chinese provenance is said to have come from Shansi.[2]

A site which has been explored by Dr. Nils Palmgren is Ch'ing-ho-hsien, some hundred miles to the west of Tz'ŭ-chou itself, which was partly abandoned after a flood, like Chü-lu-hsien. His material comes from graves between the older and the later city walls and he considers that the great majority is of Sung date. But it included a little primitive blue-and-white as well as the more developed type of enamelled Tz'ŭ-chou ware mentioned above, decorated with black, brown, green, rust red and yellow or yellow-green.[3] The other Tz'ŭ-chou types were represented in his finds but no wasters or other evidence of kilns. Two of the more striking pieces from this site are a vase with black slip 'inlaid' in white slip, the two being kept apart by incised lines,[4] and a foliate vase painted with a floral spray on white slip under a green glaze.[5] This latter kind is uncommon but there is a vase in the British Museum and a wine ewer in the Victoria and Albert with the addition of ferruginous spots on the handle, similar to those noted on Ting-yao. Another northern site where large numbers of shards have been found but at present no definite evidence of kilns, is Chiao-tso in Northern Honan, visited by Mr. Orvar Karlbeck in 1934 and in 1943 by Mr. Koyama, who prefers to call it Wu-hsiao, the name of the Department in which it lies. It seems not to be a big habitation site and the mass of pottery fragments do probably point to kilns. The two main types of ware represented are Tz'ŭ-chou and Black wares. Like Dr. Palmgren, Mr. Koyama seems confident in being able to identify pieces with no history as products of these kilns. Although he is not explicit in his stylistic analysis he would appear to attribute to Chiao Tso (Wu hsiao) many of the finest pieces of Tz'ŭ-chou type, whether incised, carved or painted, including the green glazed kind represented by the Eumorfopoulos vase (1). It is hard to believe that, in the present state of our knowledge of the North China kiln sites, it is possible to discriminate between the products of different kilns—the examination even of the sites visited has been too hurried and partial; so that it

[1] *Toji*, vol. V, no. 3, July 1933 for another example in Japan. There were four pieces in the Eumorfopoulos collection.

[2] W. Hochstädter, Buffalo Museum, fig. 96.

[3] *Nordlik Sung-Keramik en Svenska Samlingar*, National Museum, Stockholm, 1949, p. 34.

[4] ibid. p. 13.   [5] ibid. p. 14.

(1) *Colour Plate* B.

seems better to wait for more thorough surveys and to hold to the well-understood classification by type. At the same time it is pertinent to recall that Hobson wrote in 1937[1] the distinction between Ting types, Tz'ŭ-chou types and Northern Black Wares (or *Temmoku*) is not well marked, and that it is probable that all three types were made in the same kiln centres.

It is necessary now to make a brief excursion to one of the southern kiln centres, in Fukien, before continuing the account of the Northern wares in the Sung period. There is a large group of wares classed by the Chinese as 'black' glazed although the glaze is usually a very dark brown often streaked with a deep lustrous blue and flecked with a warm tawny brown, shading at the mouth, which is usually bare of glaze, to a golden brown. Sometimes, however, especially in the southern group, the glaze is a uniform dense gall-colour. All these effects are obtained with iron. It seems certain that these glazes were first used on the dark Fukien body for tea bowls, and not before Sung, for under T'ang it has been seen that green Yüeh-yao or white Hsing-yao were the types esteemed by tea drinkers. The tea bowls were probably first made in the north part of Fukien province in the Chien-ning district in the tenth century—the body is very dark, a purplish brown after firing, and the bowls are mostly deep and rather straight-sided. The glaze is thick and stops well short of the base but has usually run down irregularly. It is very dark but seldom quite black and is often marked with streaks of blue and brown likened by the Chinese to hare's fur. The lustrous effect is due to the presence of minute bubbles in the glaze. This Chien ware reached Japan from the kilns, which are some sixty to seventy miles from the coast, and this kind of bowl was highly esteemed for its colour and potting when the cult of tea drinking was developed in the twelfth century. It was then known as *Temmoku*, a name apparently representing the Chinese T'ien-mu, a mountain said by Pelliot to be not in Fukien but Chekiang, near Hangchow, from where these wares may well have been shipped to Japan. The Japanese have treasured some of the Sung Chien-yao bowls and it was by this name of Temmoku that the type was for long known in the West. In 1935 some large kiln waste hills were discovered in North Fukien by J. M. Plumer, 30 miles due north of Chien-ning-fu, containing thousands of imperfect bowls of the Chien ware. In Fukien in the Sung period only tea-bowls were made in this black glazed ware. Sometimes these are very large, and the largest recorded now in the Percival David Foundation is no less than 10·3

---

[1] Handbook, pp. 36, 38. Hobson mentions ' a considerable industry' at Chiao Tso. In the British Museum are fragments of Chün as well as Tz'ŭ-chou and Black ware from this neighbourhood, see p. 32 below and B.M.Q. VIII, pp. 70–71.

inches in diameter. The rim is sheathed in silver which is reputed to be an original Sung mount.

This Chien ware was soon imitated in other provinces, especially Honan, Chihli and Kiangsi. In the north the iron black glaze was extensively used in the Northern Sung period. It seems to have been made in a number of different localities, probably generally associated with Tz'ŭ-chou types. Indeed the Japanese now tend to distribute these black wares between Ting types and Tz'ŭ-chou types in accordance with the hardness and whiteness of the body. If it is hard and porcellanous the piece is classed with Ting-yao; if it is a stone ware it is classed with the Tz'ŭ-chou. Since however these names have already to do duty for a number of different types it seems better to retain a separate name for this type until at least all the kiln sites have been located and thoroughly examined. After all they have in common their derivation from the southern black ware of Chien-ning, and like celadon this colour-name is convenient and clear. So for instance the black ware found by Koyama at Chiao-tso or Wu-hsiao near the northern capital K'ai-fêng and called by him 'black Ting' will here be treated with the other black glazed wares. It seems likely that the harder-bodied, more porcellanous black glazed wares were made in Honan, as Hobson suggested in 1935 in the David Catalogue.[1] The Chihli types of Black-ware are very varied and a great range has been found at the sites of Chü-lu-hsien and Ch'ing-ho. The body ranges from a grey buff to near-white stoneware, and the best shapes are the high-shouldered vases with small neck and rather narrow foot, and the round-bodied vases with flaring wide mouth (1). A particularly interesting effect is obtained by applying narrow strips of slip under the glaze which appear as ribs strengthening the form (2). So too the variegation of the brown marking was much more exploited by potters in the North who found ways of controlling them, perhaps by mixing a glaze containing oxide in the glaze in greater or less quantity,[2] so that wide partings of brown and black are common. A much rarer effect of reaction of the glaze during firing is to cover the vessel with constellations of silver spots. They are caused by the bursting of bubbles in the glaze, leaving crystals on the surface. This beautiful effect has been given the unpoetic name of 'oil-spot' (3). A unique[3] example of a similar effect but in bright red

---

[1] P. XXX 'Black glaze . . . was used . . . at the Honan factories which have a white porcellanous body, albeit sometimes dressed with a wash of black clay'.

[2] A. L. Hetherington, *Chinese Ceramic Glazes*, 1937, pp. 29-30.

[3] Unless this is referred to by Dr. Palmgren, *op. cit.*, p. 35 as 'light copper red'.

---

(1) *Plates* 62, 66; (2) *Plate* 65; (3) *Plate* 61.

is now in the Fitzwilliam Museum, Cambridge (1), as part of the Oscar Raphael bequest. It should however be remarked that this bowl has been repaired in Japan and that some of the spots, which are much larger than the oil spots, are additions painted on there to hide the repair. Actual overglaze painting is occasionally found on these northern black pieces. A vase with overglaze painting in white and colour entered the British Museum with the Oppenheim collection, and Koyama reproduces a bowl painted with gold flowers. Similar painting in gold occurs on a black bowl found in a Koryu tomb[1] to which Hobson has compared a black bowl in the David Collection[2] which has been called 'Black Ting', but which does not appear to have a true Ting body. Such gold or colour painting may have been a subsequent addition not executed at the kiln.

Is it possible to say when these Northern black wares ceased? A tall vase in the David Foundation[3] was attributed by Hobson to the sixteenth century, but the splayed foot and well-marked mouth suggest a much earlier date; and in spite of the body clearly seen at the dressed foot, an attribution to the Sung period seems justified. It is possible that the shape is derived from a Persian metal vase such as the silver flasks of the eleventh or twelth century date.[4] Certainly the splayed foot, though it is only slightly hollow, suggests a metal derivation. The swelling body is however truly ceramic. There is in fact no reason to think that production of these black wares continued beyond the end of the Sung period.

It remains to mention the Black wares of Kiangsi centred round the kiln centre of Kian (Chi-an fu). The body of this ware is a light grey which burns a saffron colour, and it is sometimes covered with a wash of dark slip, evidently in imitation of Chien-yao. The glaze lacks the lustre of the other Black wares described above, but the finer pieces, such as a tripod incense burner in the British Museum (Eumorfopoulos Collection) have a distinctive and successful marking like snake-skin or palm trunk. In fact the outstanding quality of the Kian wares is the power to control the kiln transformations of the glaze so as to produce designs, often of birds or flowers, or all-over patterns such as are not found on any of the northern wares. A special effect is obtained by placing a leaf on the bowl in the kiln which bears its imprint in the glaze where it has partly protected it before its consumption. A good

[1] *Chosen Koseki Zufu*, VIII, No. 3740.

[2] *Catalogue* plate LXXXIII.

[3] Chinese Exhibition 1935, No. 1212, cf. Hobson *Wares of the Ming Dynasty*, pl. 74.

[4] Smirnov, *Argenterie Orientale*, pl. LXXXIII.

(1) *Plate* 60.

series of examples of this ware are in the Charles B. Hoyt Collection in the Museum of Fine Arts, Boston;[1] and Brankston brought back some bowls and fragments from the nearby site of Yung-ho (Chi-chou) which are now in the British Museum. This does not exhaust the list of kiln centres of black ware,[2] but an idea has been given of their range and variety.

It is now proposed to describe the other principal Northern wares of the Sung dynasty. In Northern Honan, south of the Yellow River and not very far to the south-west of K'ai-fêng, the Northern Sung capital, lay Chün-chou, in Yü-hsien. It has given its name to a well-known class of blue glazed wares which were certainly made in that neighbourhood, for many kiln-sites have been discovered in this part of northern Honan on which fragments and wasters of this type are common.[3] As will be shewn the ware certainly goes back to the Northern Sung dynasty, and it seems to be the basic type from which the classic ware of the Ju-yao, as well perhaps as the at present unidentified Ch'ai, derive. On the other hand it is certain that production continued at some of the kilns down to the Ming period, quite apart from imitations made elsewhere in China at that time. Yet the great number of the surviving pieces form a consistent group with a grey-buff body, usually dressed on the base with a brown slip which varies from a warm yellow-brown to a cold grey-brown, and thickly glazed with an opalescent blue glaze. This blue is due to the iron content of the glaze, but analysis shows that this amounts to only about 1·6 to 2·5 per cent. The foot rim is never glazed but the rest including the base is usually glazed. Some large flower pots have a bare lip and were presumably fired resting on it, but in all other shapes the glaze has run down viscously until it collects in big drops near the base. On an ink-slab in the British Museum the glaze forms 'feet' at two of the corners, so thick is it. Some channels appear in the glaze, probably owing to its intractability, and are known to the modern Chinese as 'worm-tracks' but more notable are the many pin-holes produced by the bursting of bubbles in the glaze. The most striking feature of many of the Chün products is the purple or crimson splashing and mottling, due to the oxidizing of copper in the glaze. A very small amount of copper would be sufficient to produce this effect, and it is more probable that this was added locally to the body rather than blown on to the glaze on the turntables as had been suggested. But this is not a universal feature, as some of the finer pieces are without it (1). It is however always found

[1] Nos. 323–331.   [2] Dr. Palmgren attributes a group to kilns in Shensi.

[3] A series of fragments from various sites in Honan was presented to the British Museum in 1934 by Sir Percival David.

(1) *Plate* 84.

in the most famous, if not the most attractive products of the Chün kilns, the 'numbered' flower-pots and bulb-bowls. These are always deeply suffused with red on the outside, but the inside surface, which was less exposed to the air draughts in the kiln, is usually a plain lavender blue. The numbers (one to ten) are found incised under the slip on the base. It has been suggested that they refer to sizes; but a survey of the considerable number of published pieces does not support this view. It rather suggests that some scale of shapes is the more likely explanation. For instance, at least three bulb-bowls (of the shape in the British Museum *Handbook* fig. 41) are numbered '7', but then two others in the David Collection are numbered 4 and 5: a square flower pot in the British Museum and the corresponding square stand in the Schiller Collection are both numbered '10'. Three six-lobed bulb-bowls are numbered '9', but one is numbered '8'. Do they perhaps belong to *sets* of different shapes, made up in numbered series?[1] In the fifteenth century the Court we know to have received this type of object from the Chün kilns.[2] These bulb-bowls, unlike the other Chun pieces, seem always to have been fired standing on a ring of twenty or so spurs which have left marks on the base. Some of these flower pots suggest by their shapes the Ming three-coloured wares, and if these start in the fifteenth century it may be that they were the successors of the Chün flower-pots and bulb-bowls which themselves may be not very much earlier. Dr. J. C. Ferguson suggests that the numbers correspond to numbers given to test pieces graded by colour. But test pieces collected at the kilns at Chiao Tso in N. Honan and now in the British Museum are not marked with numbers but with symbols.

Some of the finer pieces do not show the flambé effects but are crackled. They are to be distinguished from the less porcellanous, coarse-bodied pieces. A finer crackle appears in the less refractory glaze of the soft-bodied Ma Chün which seems to extend from Southern Sung to the Ming period. Chün types were much imitated both in Kuangtung province and also at Ihing in Kiangsu at the mouth of the Yangtze where a potter named Ou of the later Ming period was especially successful in making copies.

[1] On numbered Chün see Bosch Reitz, 1916, Appendix, and George Lee in O.C.S. Transactions Vol. 21 (1945–6). His suggestion that the flambé effects were due to copper particles blown on while the vessel was on the turntable will not hold, for analysis by Mr. K. Shinobu, translated and published in the *Far Eastern Ceramic Bulletin*, September 1950, has shown no significant copper content.

[2] The K'ang-hsi *Encyclopaedia* records the imperial use of Chün flower pots in the Hsüan-te period. There appears to be no evidence for earlier supply of Chün-yao to the Court.

One of the most characteristic of Chün shapes is a jar with two small ear-handles by the short neck (cf. the Eumorfopoulos example, Chinese exhibition No. 1083). Of similar shape but with a green glaze is a jar in the British Museum (1). Fragments of green Chün have been found at Lin-ao-chen, west of Pao Fêng, Honan. This green Chün has a denser glaze than celadon and tends to grey rather than brown or blue: the colour may be compared to the skin of an almond.

Perhaps the finest of all Chün wares are those which may have been made for the scholar's table, water pots, shallow dishes of foliate form or with flanged edges, small boxes. Although these have not the perfection of shape or glaze later reached in the Southern Sung Kuan ware or Lung-ch'üan, they have a similar appeal to the sense of touch and depend upon the play of light over the glaze in a way that Ting-yao does not. They have the warmth of a Renoir as against the fine line of an Ingres.

In fact these Chün products may be deemed to have set the line for the later classic wares of Kuan and Ko. The early date of the ware is supported by the find of Chün fragments on sites of the Liao period (A.D. 907–1124) in Manchuria, in which context also Ting and Tzü-chou fragments were found by Japanese excavators. Many kiln sites strewn with fragments and wasters have been found in Northern Honan, and it is probable that manufacture of Chün wares was general in the area a hundred miles round Honan-fu. The 'stagnant' quality of the glaze has been remarked; this appearance is due to opacity. Analyses by Mr. Hetherington and Mr. K. Shinobu have shown that this is the result of a substantial quantity of phosphates in suspension in the glaze.

Unquestionably the Ju-chou neighbourhood which lies not far to the west of Chün-chou, contained kilns of the ware commonly known as 'Northern celadon'.[1] And the Japanese, followed by some American writers, would prefer to use *Ju-yao* as a geographical term to cover all wares made in this Ju-chou district of western Honan or at least the Northern Celadon which is the most plentiful. Since however the name is that of one of the 'classic' wares mentioned in the Chinese texts at least as early as A.D. 1124, which has moreover been convincingly identified from the descriptions by Sir Percival David[2]

[1] See Hobson in O.C.S. *Transactions* vol. 14, 1936–7, discussing fragments of this ware sent to the British Museum by Nakao and others. Brankston, *Early Wares of Chingtehen*, p. 101, gives the neighbourhood of Sian in Shensi as the kiln centre for Northern Celadon.

[2] P. David in O.C.S. *Transactions*, vol. 14, p. 20.

---

(1) *Plate* 83.

who has exhaustively studied the evidence, Hobson wished to confine the use of the name Ju-yao to the imperial ware made in the Ju-chou district between the years 1107 and 1127 only, in the last days of the Northern Sung capital of Kai-fêng, nearby. This is the practice which has general acceptance in England which is fortunate to be the guardian of about a dozen pieces of this rare ware, and it is followed in his book. It must however be expected that a kind of Ju-yao ware was made at Ju-chou before the classic ware, and this is likely to have resembled Chun-yao—Count Otani went so far as to consider the earlier Ju-yao as 'Northern Kuan'—the identification of this has already been touched upon and it has been mentioned that Sir Percival David suggested the identity of Northern Kuan with the *classic* Ju-yao. Here it must be added that some Chinese scholars have attributed all Kuan pieces (using the latter word in its general sense) with a buff body, to the North, but there seem to be undoubtedly Southern Kuan pieces with light bodies. There are in several collections pieces of Ju type resembling the classic Ju in glaze but lacking its finer quality, and these may perhaps be precursors of work produced at the kilns after the departure of the court. Of this kind is a vase with spur marks in the Herbert Ingram Collection and a larger saucer dish in the British Museum, with an exposed foot rim and smaller areas left exposed in the firing burnt red. In any case if the Chün-yao kilns started to produce their characteristic wares early in the Sung period there is time for them to have evolved the Ju type by 1107 when the imperial kiln is said to have started.

Ju-yao is a buff or pinkish-yellow stoneware with a smooth dense greenish-blue (duck's egg) glaze, intractable but well-controlled. Generally the whole vessel is covered by this glaze. It is sometimes but not always crackled, and appears with all its fineness to be an experimental ware. If the inscribed ring in the Percival David Foundation is to be relied on, the imperial factory was started in 1107 so that the life was only twenty years, before the end of the Northern Sung period; and there is no Southern Ju-yao. In spite of these facts any sensitive person who is privileged to study and handle the group of Ju pieces in the Percival David Foundation will become convinced of the consistency of this type with its glaze distinguished by a gem-like quality, not opalescent like Chün, nor unctuous like the Southern Kuan or Lung-ch'üan wares, but both clear and refractory. The finest pieces are perhaps the two oval brush-washers but these two differ in quality of glaze. The cup-stand here reproduced for the first time by kind permission of the fortunate owner Sir Harry Garner (1), clearly

---

(1) *Colour Plate* C.

resembles one in the Percival David Foundation,[1] yet it is by no means identical in glaze, has a bare-foot with no spur marks and the lotus leaf shape is more clearly defined. It may be added in passing that this shape occurs also in Northern black ware,[2] and in Northern Celadon found in Koryu tombs,[3] and lacquer found at Chü-lu-hsien, and is possibly originally a silver form. It is the remote ancestor of the western cup and saucer. Like all the shapes occurring in Ju-yao it is truly ceramic, uninfluenced by the bronze tradition, and the potting is of the finest, the quality can therefore be only fully appreciated by handling: its sensuous nature is typical of the aesthetic and liberal spirit of the court of Hui-tsung which was so rudely interrupted by the Chin invaders in 1126.

The ware was highly appreciated by that connoisseur the emperor Ch'ien Lung and a number of appreciative poems were composed by him for inscribing on the bases of pieces in his collection. Of these a bowl in the David Foundation[4] has a fine sensitive shape which is emphasized by the crackle which gathers especially below the rim. This is sheathed in copper presumably to protect a damaged edge for it was fired on the spurs which was usual in this ware. In the British Museum are two saucer dishes inscribed in the same way. Both are from the Eumorfopoulos Collection and both were involved in a fire in the Imperial palace which has discoloured the glaze with fresh transmutations. One of these has a lip curving inwards and a foot rim splayed outwards like the David bowl, and the buff body is visible at the five spur-marks on the base. The glaze seems originally to have been a slightly lavender blue and is uncrackled. The second piece has a double crackle and was probably a paler and purer blue 'of the sky after rain' but it has also the same body and five spur marks. These are also found in the foot of the third example in the Museum, happily undamaged, a more elegant saucer dish with delicate slightly foliate rim.

Northern celadon was probably made at several kiln centres in Honan, one of which has been located by finds of wasters at Ta-ying-chou, about 20 li from Ju-chou. Some of these are in the British Museum. They show foliate shapes, are decorated with carving and moulds. All the northern wares have particulars of shape and decoration in common, but a special link has been noted between the Northern celadon and some of the Ying-ch'ing.[5] This is natural, for in both wares carving and combing were extensively used with freedom. The northern

---

[1] Hobson, *Catalogue* pl. IV.

[2] Siren, 3,000 Years, II, pp. 384, 389. A Chün-yao cup in the Barlow collection is also similar.

[3] Prince Yi Museum Catalogue, 1932, pl. 29.

[4] Hobson, *Catalogue*, pl. II; Honey, pl. 40B.   [5] Hobson, *Handbook*, p. 25.

C. Cup stand. Diameter 6½ in. Ju-yao. Sung dynasty.
Sir Harry Garner
See page 35

celadon is the finer ware, and the design is more firmly handled to suggest cloud or wave background as in a beautiful little bowl in the British Museum with shells in the centre (1). This is from Chü-lu-hsien, where *Ying-ch'ing* has also been found. Both wares also show as a favourite decorative motif radiating strokes on the under-sides of bowls. Just as close as a matter of fact is the link between Northern celadon and Ting-yao, especially in the carved floral designs and in the use of moulds. In the celadon the potting is heavier and the darker glaze calls for a high relief in the carving of the body while in Ting-yao naturally more use is made of the beauty of the potting below the colourless glaze. On the other hand the descent of northern celadon from Yüeh-yao is clear, for it shares with it not only the glaze colour (which of course was imitated from Yüeh-yao in many parts of China) but also the practice of firing on little rings of clay or sand traces of which are found adhering to the base in both wares. In shape too and decoration it is easy to see this connection. Such Yüeh-yao vessels as those reproduced in plates 16 and 19 clearly foreshadow well-known types of northern celadon. The frieze of petals round the base which has been noted as characteristic of Yüeh-yao is not uncommon in northern celadon, and the brocade character of all-over decoration, generally peony or chrysanthemum scrolls, is another legacy of the Yüeh kilns. It is to be noted in this connection that there is no such close relation between Lung-ch'üan and Yüeh-yao is spite of the fact that these kilns were both in Chekiang, though certainly at opposite ends of the province. A hiatus in time is the only credible explanation of their disparity in style.

One other connection of northern celadon must be noted, that in glaze with the Koryu celadons of Korea. The earliest of these wares do indeed suggest a direct connection with the incised tenth century Yüeh-yao as was remarked by Hsü Ching on his visit in 1124, but as would be expected the links with the northern Chinese wares are closer and more constant. Indeed it would sometimes be difficult to distinguish the Koryu celadons from northern celadon were it not that they are fired on spurs which have left their characteristic marks on the base, instead of on clay heaps. The body in each case is grey, burning red if exposed in the kiln, but in the Chinese ware there is a much greater range of colour in the glaze from an olive green to a greyish blue. It is strange that this distinguished and beautiful ware should not have won notice from Chinese writers on ceramics, and it is therefore tempting to identify it with *Tung-yao* mentioned in the *Ko-Ku-Yao-Lun* as a northern Honan product. But this and other references

---

(1) *Plate* 67.

suggest a rarer ware than the northern celadon and attempts have been made to identify it with the Alexander bowl in the British Museum mentioned above,[1] with an ewer in the National Museum, Tokyo,[2] and a somewhat similar ewer in the Hoyt Collection.[3] Neither of these last appears to have any particular history and they seem to be examples from one of the northern celadon kilns not much different from many others.[4] On the other hand a bottle (1) in the Percival David Foundation has a finely crackled green glaze over a light body with a dark wash, remarkably light in weight, of fine quality. This is certainly a rare type though there are comparable pieces in the Barlow and Clark Collections. There is equally no special reason to connect this ware with Tung-yao, but it corresponds with the passage from the *Ko-Ku-Yao-Lun* quoted in the *T'ao Shuo* (Bushell, p. 49), 'it is of pale green colour marked with fine crackle lines', and it is a northern piece of fine quality, which has been in the Imperial Collection, but[5] the true Tung-yao central type can only be picked out with certainty when the kiln site may have been found and thoroughly investigated.

[1] Cf. p. 18; Hobson, *Handbook*, pp. 24–5, fig. 40.
[2] G. St. G. M. Gompertz, in *Oriental Art*, vol. III, No. 3, p. 123, fig. 4.
[3] Memorial catalogue, fig. no. 229.   [4] Cf. Honey, p. 37A.
[5] In 1790 Ch'ien-lung had a commendation inscribed on the base, but this does not refer to *Tung*.

(1) *Plate* 96.

6

THE SOUTHERN SUNG AND YÜAN PERIODS

In the discussion of the Northern wares some reference to the Southern Sung period has already been made in relation to both Ting-yao and to the Kuan wares. It has been suggested that Kuan probably was not used in an exclusive sense of the products of a single factory or kiln-centre in the Sung period, but only acquired this more precise and restricted meaning at a later date. However in accordance with the commonsense view that it is best to retain accepted nomenclature wherever possible, it is proposed here to use Kuan to mean the group of southern Sung wares which were made in the neighbourhood of the new capital at Hangchow at several kiln centres, not all of which have been discovered.

According to the tradition the first imperial factory at Hangchow was established at the Surveyor's Office, or *Hsiu-nei-ssŭ*, on Phoenix Hill, but not long afterwards it was moved to a spot near the Altar of Heaven, or *Ch'iao-tan*. The latter kiln site was definitely located by two Japanese ceramic students Kozui Otani and Dr. Nakao. Subsequently Hobson also visited the site and picked up fragments of a dark bodied ware with pale blue-green glaze, so thinly potted that the body is less than the glaze on either side of it, as may be seen in the reproduction of a damaged dish in Sir Harry Garner's collection (1). The glaze is crackled and is unctuous and not readily fusible. Fortunately something more survives than fragments and it has been possible to identify a small number of whole pieces of this distinguished ware.

Hobson identified from the fragments a flask-shaped vase now in the British Museum (Eumorfopoulos Collection),[1] which has an irregularly crackled glaze and dark body. It is a beautiful piece to handle, and it shows the indescribable depth and opacity of the vitrified glaze. This opacity was attributed by Mr. Hetherington to the presence of phosphorus, forming a ferrous phosphate with the iron, to which of course it owes its colour. But an analysis of fragments from the site carried

---

[1] *Handbook*, fig. 34.

---

(1) *Plate* 85B.

out at the instance of Sir Harry Garner has shown that there is actually no phosphorus present in either glaze or body, but that the opacity is due in fact to the presence of minute particles of lime in suspension in the glaze. Lime (calcium oxide) is also present in appreciable quantity in both Chün-yao and Lung-ch'üan celadon, but only in about half the proportion found in the Kuan-yao. The Kuan pieces have a wide range of colour from the rather watery green of the Museum vase, through an intense lavender blue of a bronze-shape (*Ku*) vase sent by the Chinese Government to the 1935 Exhibition,[1] and the grey blue of an excavated piece from a grave in Chekiang (1), to the whitish glaze of another vase from the Eumorfopoulos Collection now in the British Museum.[2] This beautiful piece has a much larger crackle and the glaze is so intractable that it has formed perceptible ridges and runs on the body, yet is of a marvellous smooth opacity. Hobson suggested that this might represent the Phoenix Hill kiln, but Sir Percival David is inclined to see the best controlled pieces like the hexagonal brush washer in his collection or the similar Palace piece as the work of this earlier kiln.[3] At present there is no means of knowing, but it is worth remarking that it seems to have been this type especially which was copied at Ching-tê-chên in the eighteenth century.[4] Unfortunately there are not only those imitations, of wonderful quality, to distinguish from the originals, (there are several with Yung chêng marks not erased to help in this), but there are other 'Kuan types', which have great quality, yet must be from other kilns for they have a light body. For instance there is another bronze-shaped piece in the David Foundation[5] with a thick, vitrified, rather bubbly glaze of Kuan type, but a light body and light in weight. Is this a northern ware, or is it from some other Chekiang kiln centre? In addition to the Kuan fragments found by Dr. Nakao at Hangchow, he reported fragments of a celadon with a 'greyish-white porcelain body'. This type of ware is usually referred to as 'Hangchow celadon': the glaze is nearer to Kuan than to Lung-ch'üan.

A further problem must now be discussed and that is the identity of *Ko* ware. This was traditionally supposed to be a fine black-bodied ware made at Lung-ch'üan by the elder (*Ko*) of two famous brothers of the name of Chang. But no black-bodied ware seems to have been made at Lung-ch'üan, and the type called *Ko-yao* by the Palace authorities is

---

[1] Catalogue of Chinese Govt. Exhibition No. 30: *Ku Kung* IV, 4.
[2] *Handbook*, fig. 32; Honey, pl. 40A. [3] *Catalogue*, pl. IX.
[4] Cf. R. S. Jenyns, *Later Chinese Porcelain*, pl. LXIV.
[5] No. 9.

(1) *Plate 86.*

not clearly distinguishable by specific criteria from Kuan-yao.[1] It tends to have a more regular and conspicuous crackle, and the glaze to be white and denser owing to a greater number of bubbles; but these are variants that can occur in the same kiln, and this may be only a fanciful name for a particular effect found in Kuan ware. If so, it covers the most delicate and precious of the Kuan pieces and when copied in the eighteenth century, oversweet and artificial.[2] But a few pieces convince one of their authenticity and of their soundness, for instance an incense burner with wing handles, once in the Eumor-fopoulos Collection (1), and now in the Percival David Foundation.

The most important celadon kilns of the southern Sung period, in productivity and perhaps also in aesthetic quality are, however, those of Lung-ch'üan at the opposite, southern extreme of Chekiang province in Ch'u-chou prefecture, towards the Fukien border. Although this ware took the place of the earlier Chekiang celadons of Yüeh-chou as a leading export, it cannot be said that there was any direct contact, for the Lung-ch'üan kilns cannot be shown to go back, as will be explained, as far as the tenth century. The body is a much whiter grey than that of Yüeh-yao and it burns a saffron colour when exposed to the draught of the kiln. The glaze is considerably less tractable, and is more viscous. The colour varies from a rare leaf-green to the more usual cold bluish-green that is due entirely to iron and not as has been suggested to oxide of cobalt, although the glaze contains only about one per cent of iron oxide. It is sometimes crackled, but always with a wide and irregular pattern, as in the beautiful pair of bottles belonging to Sir Alan Barlow, of which one is reproduced in colour (2). In this it differs from the Hangchow celadons, which are usually heavily crackled. The effect of crackle was evidently much admired under the Sung, and the potters of this period quickly learned how to exploit what was probably at first an accidental effect of firing so thick a glaze at so high a temperature. The different pace of contraction of body and glaze produces 'ice-cracks', and for this reason they are related in general direction to the shape of the vessel, the plastic quality of which they thus emphasise. An all-over crackle, particularly if accompanied by a secondary crazing, as in the *Ko* type especially, has

[1] It is however possible that the black body of Kuan and Ko was an artificial product and so as rare as the imperial pieces themselves.

[2] Cf. Catalogue of Chinese Govt. Exhibits, vol. II, Nos. 253–4.

---

(1) *Plate* 87A; (2) *Colour Plate* D. This shape is also found in Kuan-yao e.g. Chinese Government Exhibits, vol. II, No. 28 and an example from Sir Daniel Hall's collection, now belonging to Mr. R. C. Bruce. Both these have a large crackle.

an effect rather of accentuating the depth of the glaze, its opaqueness or refraction of light. The finest Lung-ch'üan (1) which the Japanese call *Kinuta*, after a famous mallet-shaped vase, absorbs the light into its deep and mysterious glaze, through which the ribs of the form, or the occasional moulded design (as on a beautiful rounded box in the Oppenheim Collection, British Museum) show lighter. Many of the pieces in our collections to-day, were rejected by the Sung potters because they fell short of the exacting standards of their day, but appear to us hardly blemished. Others which are clear wasters still possess great quality—because of the sheer beauty of the glaze. A rare variety of Lung-ch'üan generally known by the Japanese name of Tobi Seiji (buckwheat celadon), has ferruginous spots of brown where iron is in excess. Examples are in the Percival David Foundation[1] and the Victoria and Albert Museum.[2]

Shapes of Lung-ch'üan are usually simple flat dishes, conical bowls, deep bowls with lotus petals carved outside, small vases with flaring mouths, sometimes with attached ring handles. But the shapes include several which are ceramic modifications of archaic bronze forms. The tripod incense burner (*ting*) with partly hollow legs; the two ear-handled *kuei*; the *kinuta* shape itself (2), with moulded fish or phoenix handles and sharply everted lip; and also the octagonal bottle with its pierced high foot, are clearly all derived from metal prototypes, although not all from early ritual bronzes. A more monumental shape is derived from the jade cylinder *ts'ung*, but adapted to serve as a flower vase. All these forms have been subtly modified by the potters who have retained the essence of their 'high-birth', while the cut and texture of their ceramic dress gives them intimate sensuous grace. The heavier pieces from the Lung-ch'üan kilns, are bulb-bowls, large dishes and jars; and these are often decorated with moulded designs, the relief being often left bare of glaze in the biscuit. Although these shapes originate in the Sung period, most examples are of later date, Yüan or early Ming.

The dates both of the beginning and the end of the activity of the Lung-ch'üan kilns are unknown. Unfortunately the finding of a few small fragments of the ware in the palace quarter of Samarra[3] on the Tigris is not conclusive evidence of a ninth century date. As has already been mentioned in connection with the northern white wares, the departure of the Caliph's court did not at once reduce Samarra to

[1] *Catalogue*, plate LV.　　　　　　　　　　[2] Honey, plate 36A.

[3] F. Sarre, *Die Keramik von Samarra*, Taf. XXIII (11, 12) and 'Excavations at Samarra, 1936–9', published by the Iraq Dept. of Antiquities, 1940, Plate CII.

(1) *Plate* 90; (2) *Plate* 90.

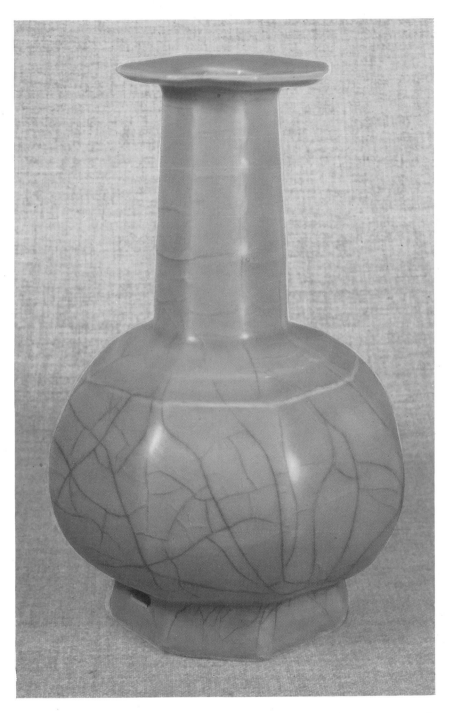

D. *Octagonal vase with crackled glaze. Lung-ch'üan celadon. Ht. 8$\frac{3}{8}$ in.*
Sung dynasty. Sir Alan Barlow, Bt., G.C.B.
See page 40

insignificance. No fragments have been found at Susa nor at Brahmin-abad in Sind, nor even at Chü-lu-hsien. On the other hand finds of fragments have been plentiful at Fostât, the Fatimid capital of Egypt, but its occurrence on this unstratified site and its copying in a local product do not carry it back necessarily beyond the twelfth century, if they confirm its wide renown. No doubt it was the products of these kilns which were presented by Saladin to the Sultan of Damascus in 1171, and thousands of shards picked up on the beach of Kamakura in southern Japan witness to another export market which they served. Pieces of the type have been found in supposedly Liao dynasty levels at Chung-ching in Manchuria,[1] but none of these finds can support the Chinese tradition that these kilns were operating in the Northern Sung period. And it must be added that the tradition of the 'removal' of the kilns at the beginning of Ming to the prefectural capital of Ch'u-chou is equally unsupported. At any rate the kilns at Lung-ch'üan appear to have been particularly active in the Yüan period, though the finer *kinuta* type was probably no longer produced. A vase in the David Foundation[2] dated 1327 gives a good idea of the products of this kiln. The inscription under the lip mentions the Liu-hua hill where Chang is reputed to have worked. Yet this is an export piece.

Fortunately there is no doubt what were the types of ware produced at the Lung-ch'üan kilns, for a good many wasters from this site have been brought back to find a home in western collections (1). The Japanese are more particular, but on the other hand have treasured a few unburied pieces from medieval times. But in default of reliable Sung dated pieces[3] chronology can only depend on the assessment of elusive qualities of style and shape. Yet nowhere is the spirit of Southern Sung aestheticism exemplified more clearly than in the finest Lung-ch'üan celadons. The clarity of form is clothed but not obscured by the smooth, luminous, yet mysterious glaze. Where there is decoration it emphasises the shape and enhances the beauty of the glaze by varying the light. Some of the pieces which are presumably the earlier, and may be considered twelfth century, the tall vase[4] with heavy depressed body in the David Collection or the Oppenheim *ts'ung* now in the British Museum, for example, preserve a classic monumental quality, but this gradually passes, through such pieces as the well-known phoenix-handled *kinuta* vases (2) to the more fluid

---

[1] The dynasty fell in 1125. [2] *Catalogue*, Plate LI.

[3] As Hobson remarks, a large dish in the David Collection (pl. XLVIII) marked with a *nien hao* equivalent to A.D. 1086–93 'is not a piece which convinces every-one.' It has a pale, almost olive-green glaze.

[4] *Catalogue*, pl. XLI.

(1) *Plate* 89; (2) *Plate* 90.

shapes of the thirteenth century (1). With the coming of the Yüan dynasty export becomes an important consideration for the Lung-ch'üan kilns, and this fact certainly influenced shapes as well as leading to a new emphasis on sturdiness. A long-spouted ewer in the David Collection[1] may well be intended for the Near Eastern market, and it leads on in shape easily to the early Ming White wares of the Yung-lo period.[2] It is a mistake to ignore the commercial side of Chinese ceramic production. For a thousand years ceramics have been one of the principal exports of China, and although in early periods it was a limited luxury trade, it was by the end of Sung on a considerable scale as witness the 50,000 shards of Lung-ch'üan on the beach of Kamakura, the quantities found in the Korean tombs, and the reports of all the early travellers from the West down to the time of Marco Polo.

An important Sung ware, but one that does not seem to be mentioned in literature, has a thin translucent, sugary body and a pale bluish-green glaze. It is known to modern students as *Ying-ch'ing*, which is descriptive of the glaze colour, and it seems to have been made in several different parts of China, and thence exported to many parts of the world. Fragments are found at Fostât in Egypt, in Malaya, Indo-china, Inner Mongolia, and the islands of Bali and Celebes. Mrs. Aga-Oglu argued on the contrary from the scanty remains found in the Philippines by the Michigan expedition,[3] among all the mass of blue-and-white shards, that it was too fragile a ware to be suitable for export. But an alternative interpretation of this evidence is that the *Ying-ch'ing* is an earlier ware which ceased to be made soon after the 'blue-and-white' period began. And this view is confirmed by what Brankston noted at the waste heaps of Hu-t'ien, near Ching-tê-chên. There *Ying-ch'ing* was found associated with *Shu fu* ware, which is, as will be seen shortly, a Yüan ware. At Ching-tê-chên therefore *Ying-ch'ing* appears to be a Sung and Yüan product, stopping near the threshold of the Ming period. There is even a kind of blue and white porcelain in which the *Ying-ch'ing* glaze is used to cover decoration either reserved in the blue design or executed in slip. This must almost certainly date from the fourteenth century.

Ying-ch'ing was also made in the north, and it has been found in many tombs of the Koryu period in Korea; and at Ninnaji in Japan associated with Yüeh pottery of Shang-lin type, and therefore

---

[1] *Catalogue*, plate XLV.

[2] For instance, one in the E. T. Chow Collection and our plate 91.

[3] *The Art Quarterly*, Detroit, IX, 1946, p. 315.

(1) *Plates* 91, 93.

probably dating from the tenth century. Dr. Palmgren reports its presence in the waste heaps of both Ch'ing-ho and Chü-lu-hsien in Chihli. It seems likely that this northern type of *Ying-ch'ing* has a bluer glaze than the Kiangsi type. It may be possible to distinguish this northern ware by its bolder carving and bluer glaze on a rather heavier body, but evidence is still inconclusive. However some pieces are clearly related to northern celadon, both being decorated for instance with designs of boys in foliage and spiral scrollwork.[1] On the other hand the dragons with human heads on the lobed bowl in the Bruce Collection (1) and on a large vase from the Eumorfopoulos Collection,[2] now in the British Museum, are a survival from the Yüeh-yao bowls with dragon decoration (2). The Bruce piece shows to advantage the use of the comb in the wave background, and this leads on to the scantier and finer decoration of later *Ying-ch'ing* pieces like Mrs. Seligman's six-lobed bowl (3) or a beautiful bowl in the British Museum (4).

The origin of the technique too may be sought in northern celadon, among which incised wares are not rare (5). Incised Ying-ch'ing decoration probably ends with the dotted technique perhaps executed with a roulette, which have a special quality of their own, free and graceful (6). The finest of all *Ying-ch'ing* pieces is the ovoid vase from the Eumorfopoulos Collection (7), in which the figure-of-eight flowing, yet controlled, foliage, recalls once more northern celadon (8), but has been given greater importance by the strong verticals, which divide the surface into panels, and also emphasise the beautiful swelling shape of the vase.

Evidence for early date of *Ying-ch'ing* is also provided by a large round box of this ware found in Szechwan with cash of Chin Tao (A.D. 995–7).[3] This box is now in the British Museum. In the same collection is a Ying-ch'ing stem cup with spreading bowl from Chü-lu-hsien. A very different type of stem-cup with narrow stem and everted lip decorated with applied slip under a pale blue glaze was collected by Brankston at Hu T'ien and is also now in the Museum. As already stated this type is probably of fourteenth-century date. Brown spots of ferruginous glaze are found on some Ying-ch'ing pieces, similar to those on *tobi seiji* celadon, but smaller.

[1] Compare plates 71A and 81. [2] *Catalogue*, vol VI, plate XVIII.

[3] Mr. Hochstädter believes that Ying-ch'ing is near to the legendary Ch'ai ware said to have been made at Chêng-chou, Honan, only in the year 954 but this is a pure supposition. It was once equated with Ju-yao. Dr. Koyama believes that it may go back to the Six Dynasties.

(1) *Plate* 79; (2) *Plate* 17; (3) *Plate* 76A; (4) *Plate* 78; (5) Cf. *Plate* 71B; (6) *Plate* 76B; (7) *Plate* 75; (8) Cf. *Plate* 69.

Among the early wares of the Ching-tê-chên district of Kiangsi is the *Shu-fu* ware, so called because it bears these two characters which mean 'central palace' among foliage in the relief decoration inside under a thick very pale blue glaze, quite unlike the thin icy Ying ch'ing glaze (cf. Chinese government Catalogue 1936–99). From a passage in the *Ko-ku-yao-lun* (1388) this is identified as an official ware of the Yüan period. Among marked pieces only small saucer dishes and bowls with bare bases such as two in the S. K. de Forest Collection, New York,[1] are found but some larger bowls with similar glaze and decoration but with combed designs on the outside are known (|) as well as stem cups, on which underglaze blue is occasionally added. Brankston found a fragment of typical Shu-fu ware at Nan-shan near Ching-tê-chên and this must be the neighbourhood in which it was made. A small bowl which passed with the Oppenheim Collection to the British Museum bears the *Shu-fu* mark incised under the glaze on the foot. It is decorated inside with a design in relief in slip. The paste is smoother and the everted lip has a brown dressing. In this connection it is worth noting that Brankston mentions white cups with everted lips and with brown mouth rims and moulded decoration inside, and other cups and bowls with decoration painted in slip in the Yung-lo period.[2] So it is safe to conclude that the Oppenheim '*shu-fu*' bowl may be of fourteenth century date. The piece of '*shu-fu*' cited in the *Li-tai-ming-tz'ǔ t'u p'u*[3] is also said to bear the mark incised beneath the base. The illustration shows a vase with typical *Ying-ch'ing* decoration, including dragons.

Shu-fu ware may thus have continued in the early Ming period and it leads on not only to the white but also to the blue and white wares of Ching-tê-chên. Mrs. Aga-Oglu has drawn attention to the resemblance in both shape and decoration between *shu-fu* and early Ming blue and white (*Far Eastern Ceramic Bulletin*, December 1949).

Another early kiln site in the Ch'ing-tê-chên neighbourhood, known to the Chinese in the eighteenth century, was revisited by Brankston, who obtained some fragments including kiln-wasters. He quotes a passage from the *Fou-liang hsien-chih* quoting the *T'ao-ch'eng-shih-yu-kao* (*O.C.S. Transactions*, vol. 16, p. 22) previously cited by Hobson (*Chinese Pottery and Porcelain*, I, p. 71, footnote 2) referring to the *mi-sê* (millet coloured) and *fên-ch'ing* (pale blue) glaze of the thin bodied wares of Hsiang-hu of the Sung dynasty. The fragments

[1] Reproduced by F. Perzynski in his translation of an article by Hsü Chih heng, *Burlington Magazine*, Feb., 1928, pl. B and C pp. 65–76.

[2] *Early Ming Wares of Ching-te-chen*, p. 59.

[3] Plate 21.

(|) *Plate* 95.

now at the British Museum show a ware akin to *Ying-ch'ing* but greener. The bowl here reproduced (I) can only be classed as a *Shu fu* type as it is unmarked, but it could be attributed to the Yüan dynasty from independent evidence, for it bears an inscription inside in '*Bashpa*' script, a form invented in Tibet by the great reformer P'ags-pa (1235–80), who frequently visited the Chinese[1] court of Khubilai after 1254 and promulgated this script in 1269. According to Pelliot[2] it had only an ephemeral vogue in China. A similar pair of bowls is in the collection of Sir Alan Barlow. Their shape and decoration already foreshadow the early Ming white wares with engraved or slip decoration.

[1] G. Tucci, *Tibetan Painted Scrolls*, 1949, I, p. 12.
[2] P. Pelliot, *Asia Major*, II, 1925, p. 288.

(I) *Plate 95.*

SHORT BIBLIOGRAPHY

R. L. Hobson, *Handbook of the Pottery and Porcelain of the Far East preserved in the Department of Oriental Antiquities, British Museum*. 2nd edition, 1937: reprinted 1948, as 3rd edition, with minor changes (referred to as Hobson's Handbook).

Catalogue of Chinese Pottery and Porcelain in the collection of Sir Percival David, Bart., F.S.A. London, 1934.

W. B. Honey, *The Ceramic Art of China and other countries of the Far East*. 1945 (here referred to as Honey).

Leigh Ashton and Basil Gray, *Chinese Art*, 1935. Reprinted 1952 (referred to as Ashton and Gray).

Transactions of the Oriental Ceramic Society, London, volumes 1–25. 1921–52—*In progress* (referred to as O.C.S. Transactions).

(*Oriental Ceramics*) Toji—In Japanese with English titles, vols. 1–14. Tokyo, 1927–43.

O Sirén, *Tre Årtusenden Kinas Konst*. 2 vols. Stockholm, 1940–41 (referred to as Sirén: 3,000 years).

Oriental Art. A quarterly, edited by William Cohn, vol. 1–. 1948—*In progress*.

C. B. Hoyt Collection, *Memorial Exhibition, Museum of Fine Arts, Boston*, 1952 (referred to as Hoyt Catalogue).

W. Hochstädter, *Early Chinese Ceramics in the Buffalo Museum of Science*. 1946. (Reprinted from *Hobbies*, vol. 26, no. 5).

Illustrated Catalogue of Chinese Government Exhibits for the International Exhibition of Art in London, vol. II, Porcelain, Nanking, 1936 (referred to as Chinese Government Catalogue).

The Chinese Exhibition: a commemorative catalogue of the International Exhibition of Chinese Art, Royal Academy of Arts, Nov. 1935–March 1936. London, 1936 (referred to as *Commemorative Catalogue*).

The Schiller collection of Chinese ceramics, jades and bronzes. Illustrated Catalogue. City Art Gallery. Bristol, 1948.

INDEX

INDEX

1A. *Vase with ram's horn handles and impressed chequer design.*
Traces of glaze on the shoulder. Chou dynasty. Ht. 6 in.
Mrs. B. Z. Seligman
See page 3

1B. *Vase decorated with glass paste. Chou dynasty. Ht. $3\frac{7}{8}$ in.*
Mrs. Walter Sedgwick
See page 3

2. *Covered vase with animal handles and feet, unglazed, decorated with engraved ornament in bronze style. Han dynasty. Ht. 11·6 in. The British Museum*

3. *Vase of granary shape on bear feet with pigmented decoration on a white ground. Han dynasty. Ht. 11¼ in.*

Mrs. B. Z. Seligman

See page 4

4. *Vase with moulded decoration in bronze style under a green glaze over a red body covered with white slip. (The lip is restored.) Han or Six dynasties. Ht. 9 in.*
The British Museum (Eumorfopoulos Collection)
See page 4

5. *Covered vase with loop handles of bronze shape, olive green glaze,*
on a red body. From the Chin-ts'un tombs, Lo-yang.
Late Chou dynasty. Ht. 7¾ in. Diam. 8¾ in.
William Rockhill Nelson Gallery of Art,
Kansas City
See page 4

6. *Funerary urn on a stand—green glaze, much degraded. Six
dynasties. Ht. 22½ in.*
The British Museum
See page 4

7. *Vessel decorated with a design of Wu-coins under an olive green
glaze. Yüeh-yao. 3rd century* A.D. *Ht.* $14\frac{1}{2}$ *in.
Metropolitan Museum, New York*
See page 5

8. *Vase with loop handles, the upper part glazed. Protoporcelain—
from Hsŭ-chou-fu, Kiangsu. About 3rd century* A.D. *Ht.* 9·3 *in.
The British Museum*

9. *Vase with combed decoration round the neck under a greenish-brown glaze. Protoporcelain. c. 3rd century* A.D. *Ht. 7·8 in.*
The British Museum
See page 3

10. *Tall four-handled vase with olive green glaze. Protoporcelain.*
c. 3rd century A.D. *Ht. 12 in.*
The British Museum

11. *Vase with incised decoration under a brown glaze. From Yang-chow (Kiangsu). 5th-6th century* A.D. *Ht. 7 in.*
The British Museum

12. *Vase with double-loop handles and applied animal masks under a green glaze. Yüeh-yao, from Chiu-yen. 3rd century* A.D. *Ht. 8 in.*
Sir Herbert Ingram, Bart.
See page 5

13. *Amphora with four double-loop handles richly decorated with applied ornament in Sasanian style under an olive glaze. Yüeh-yao, from Chiu-yen. Six dynasties: probably 5th century* A.D. *Ht.* 9½ *in.*
Sir Herbert Ingram, Bart.
See page 7

14. *Box with carved decoration of phoenix. Yüeh-yao, from Shang-lin-hu. T'ang dynasty. Diam.* $5\frac{1}{4}$ *in.*
Mrs. Alfred Clark
See page 14

15A. *Foliate cup on a high foot. Yüeh-yao. T'ang dynasty or 10th century. Ht. 3 in. Diam. 4½ in.*
Mrs. Alfred Clark

15B. *Box of double lotus-form. The petals incised on the base, carved in relief on the cover. Yüeh-yao. T'ang dynasty. Ht. 4⅜ in.*
Fitzwilliam Museum, Cambridge

See page 14

16. *Saucerdish with carved lotus design. Yüeh-yao. T'ang/Sung.*
Diam. 5·5 in.
Mrs. B. Z. Seligman

17A. *Bowl carved on the outside with waves and on the inside with dragons. Yüeh-yao. Probably* 10th *century. Ht.* $3\frac{5}{8}$ *in. Diam.* $6\frac{5}{8}$ *in.*
Sir Herbert Ingram, Bart.
17B. *Similar bowl. Diam.* 10·7 *in.*
Metropolitan Museum, New York
See pages 16–17

18. *Covered vase with loop handles and incised decoration. Yüeh-yao.*
Probably 10th century. Ht. 12⅜ in.
Sir Herbert Ingram, Bart.
See page 17

19. *Vase* (mei p'ing) *with carved floral decoration under an olive glaze.*
Yüeh-yao. Early Sung. Ht. 10⅝ in.
Sir Herbert Ingram, Bart.
See page 16

20. *Bowl formerly on a high foot, decorated with moulded figures of musicians in roundels, under a green glaze. T'ang dynasty, or earlier. Ht. 2 in. Diam. 3⅜ in.*
Sir Herbert Ingram, Bart.
See page 16

21. *Bowl with white glaze, from Tang-yang-yu, N. Honan. T'ang
dynasty. Diam. 5¼ in.
The British Museum
See page 13*

22A. *Oval bowl on a high foot with white glaze on a porcellanous body.*
Found about 60 miles north of K'ai-fêng-fu. T'ang dynasty. 9th
century A.D. *Ht.* 2½ *in.*
Fitzwilliam Museum, Cambridge
See pages 8, 13
22B. *Porcellanous covered jar with white glaze. T'ang dynasty.*
Ht. 5⅞ *in.*
Sir Herbert Ingram, Bart.

23. *Cup on bear supports and elephant stand. Cream glaze (degraded).*
T'ang dynasty. Ht. 7·8 in.
The British Museum
See page 11

24. *Unglazed model of a duck. Wei or early T'ang dynasty.*
Length 10 in.
Mrs. Alfred Clark
See page 7

25. *Figure of an acrobat or an actor. Unglazed. T'ang. Ht. 13½ in.*
The British Museum (Eumorfopoulos Collection)

26A. *Dwarf—unglazed. T'ang dynasty. Ht. 9·5 in.*
Mrs. B. Z. Seligman
26B. *Lady in dance pose. Unglazed. T'ang dynasty. Ht. 11 in.*
Mrs. B. Z. Seligman

27. *Lady in a cloak. Creamy white glaze. From the neighbourhood of
Honan-fu. Late T'ang dynasty. Ht. 10·7 in.
The British Museum*

28. *Figure of a lady, with three colour glazes. T'ang dynasty. Ht. 13 in.*
The British Museum

29. *Buddha seated: unglazed. Post-T'ang dynasty. Ht. 12·4 in.*
The British Museum (Eumorfopoulos Collection)

30. *Covered vase; white glaze splashed with blue, green and yellow.*
T'ang dynasty. Ht. 10·5 in.
Baron Koyata Iwasaki, Tokyo
See page 10

31. *Bowl in the form of a duck. Three-coloured ware. T'ang dynasty.*
Ht. 9·5 in.
Baron Koyata Iwasaki, Japan

32. *Dish. Three-coloured ware. T'ang dynasty. Diam. 9·8 in.*
M. Calmann
See page 8

33. *Ewer. Marbled ware. T'ang dynasty. Ht.* 4½ *in.*
Mrs. Alfred Clark
See page 14

34. *A pair of lions. Ht. 9 in. and 8 in.*

35. *Three-coloured ware. T'ang dynasty.*
Baron Koyata Iwasaki, Japan

36A. *Porcelain box with ivory white glaze. Marked: Abundance. Ting
ware. Sung dynasty. Diam. 6 in. Ht. 2¾ in.
Mrs. Alfred Clark*
36B. *Stem cup. Ting ware. Sung dynasty. Diam. 4½ in.
Mrs. Alfred Clark*

37. *Bottle. Ting ware. Sung dynasty. Ht.* 8½ *in.*
The British Museum
See page 21

38. *Covered jar, from on the site of Chü-lu-hsien. Ting ware. Ht.* $4\frac{5}{8}$ *in.*
Mrs. B. Z. Seligman
See page 21

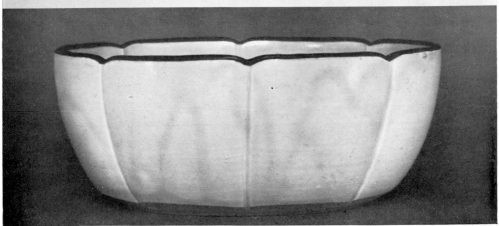

39A *and* 39B. *Lobed bowl with incised decoration inside. Ting ware.*
Sung dynasty. Diam. 8½ *in.*
Mrs. Alfred Clark
See page 21

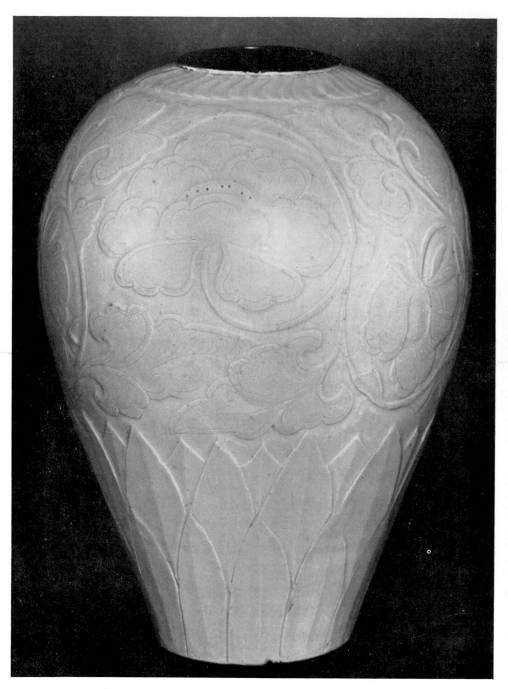

40. *Vase with carved and incised decoration. The mouth is cut down and mounted with copper. Ting ware. Sung dynasty. Ht. 12¾ in.*
Mrs. Alfred Clark

41. *Baluster vase with carved decoration. Ting ware. Sung dynasty.*
Ht. 14½ in.
The Percival David Foundation

42. *Bowl with foliate rim and incised decoration of lotuses. Ting ware.*
Sung dynasty. Diam. 8¼ in.
Mrs. B. Z. Seligman
See page 21

43. *Bowl with moulded design of phoenixes and flowers. Ting ware.*
Diam. 7 in.
The British Museum

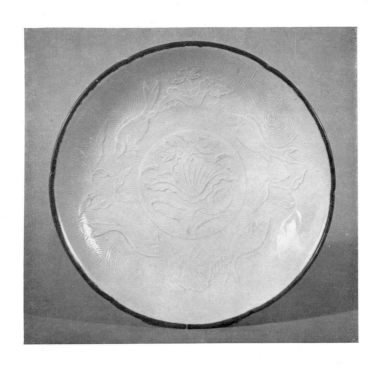

44A. *Dish with moulded design of waves and fish. Ting ware.*
Diam. 7½ in.
Fitzwilliam Museum, Cambridge
44B. *Dish with incised fish and flowers. Ting ware. Dated 1271.*
Diam. 7¾ in.
The British Museum
See page 23

45. *Dish with incised fish and waves. Ting ware. Probably
13th century. Diam. 6 in.
Fitzwilliam Museum, Cambridge*

46. *Ewer with ovoid body, and handle imitating plaited cane. Ting ware. 12th–13th century. Ht. 5½ in.*
Fitzwilliam Museum, Cambridge

47A. *Stem cup. Ting type: Southern Sung. Diam.* $4\frac{3}{8}$ *in.*
Mrs. Alfred Clark
See page 23

47B. *Waterpot with incised flowers and dragon in the round. Tu Ting*
type. Sung or later. Ht. $2\frac{1}{4}$ *in.*
Mrs. B. Z. Seligman

48. *Ewer with decayed white glaze, found on the site of Chü-lu-hsien.*
(Chihli) destroyed by flood in 1109 A.D. *Ting type. Ht.* 11¾ *in.*
Fitzwilliam Museum, Cambridge

See page 21

49. *Covered bowl, inscribed on the base in ink with the date* 1162 A.D.
Ting type. Ht. 5 *in.*
The British Museum

50. *Ovoid vase with a cream glaze, from the site of Chü-lu-hsien—*
destroyed in 1109. Ting type. Ht. 11½ in.
Fitzwilliam Museum, Cambridge
See page 21

51. *Vase with carved decoration under an olive glaze. T'zŭ-chou type.*
Sung dynasty. Ht. 15⅞ in.
Fitzwilliam Museum, Cambridge

52. *Vase with narrow mouth and painted floral decoration. T'zŭ-chou type. Ht.* 9·3 *in.*
The British Museum

53. *Brush-washer. Incised decoration. T'zŭ-chou type. Ht. 8 in.*
The British Museum
See page 24

54. *Vase painted with chrysanthemums under a golden brown glaze.*
T'zŭ-chou type. Sung dynasty. Ht. 14½ in.
Fitzwilliam Museum, Cambridge

55A. *Wine ewer with carved decoration of lotuses. T'zŭ-chou type. Sung dynasty. Ht. 5 in.*

55B. *Pillow with carved decoration and date equivalent to 1071 A.D. T'zŭ-chou type. Ht. 4½ in. Length 8·7 in.*

The British Museum

See page 24

56. *Vase with carved decoration under a grey glaze. T'zŭ-chou type.*
12th-13th century. Ht. 12·6 in.
The British Museum
See page 24

57. *Bowl enamelled on a white ground in green, red and black. T'zŭ-chou type. Sung dynasty. Ht. 3·2 in. Diam. 4½ in.*
The British Museum

58. *Saucerdish, enamelled in red, green and yellow, with a duck and
lotus design. T'zŭ-chou type. Sung dynasty. c. 1200 A.D. Diam. 8½ in.
Mrs. B. Z. Seligman
See page 25*

59. *Vase with narrow neck, painted with animals and genre scenes, in lobed panels under a turquoise blue glaze. T'zŭ-chou type. Probably 13th or 14th century. Ht. 10·7 in.*
The British Museum
See page 25

60. *Tea bowl with hare's fur blue black glaze. Chien-yao. Sung dynasty. Diam. $4\frac{1}{2}$ in.*
Mrs. Alfred Clark
See page 29

61. *Tea bowl with oil spot glaze and white slip round the lip. Northern ware. Sung dynasty. Diam. 5¾ in. × Ht. 3¼ in.*
Mrs. Alfred Clark
See page 29

62. *Globular vase, black with rust brown markings. Northern ware.*
Sung dynasty. Ht. 6 in. Diam. 7¾ in.
The British Museum (Oppenheim Collection)
See page 28

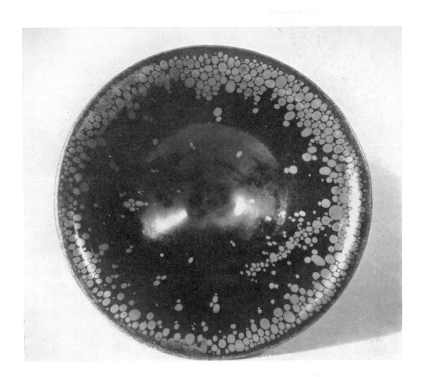

63. *Tea bowl with black glaze spotted in red, on a dark brown body.*
Repaired in Japan. Chien ware. Sung dynasty. Ht. 2½ in. Diam. 6½ in.
Fitzwilliam Museum, Cambridge

64A. *Tea bowl with mottled brown and yellow glaze. Northern ware.*
Sung dynasty. Ht. 2 in. Diam. 4¾ in.
Fitzwilliam Museum, Cambridge

64B. *Stemcup with dragon handles, pale bluish-green glaze. Ying-ch'ing*
From Honan. Sung dynasty. Ht. 3⅛ in.
Fitzwilliam Museum, Cambridge

65. *Vase with ribbed body and black glaze. Northern ware. Sung dynasty. Ht. 7·6 in.*
The British Museum
See page 28

66. *Vase with black glaze and oil spots. Northern ware. Sung dynasty.*
Ht. 10½ in.
The British Museum (Oppenheim Collection)
See page 28

67. *Bowl with incised shells and waves. From Chü-lu-hsien. Northern celadon. Sung dynasty. Diam. $5\frac{3}{4}$ in.*
The British Museum
See page 35

68. *Covered jar with incised decoration under the glaze. Northern
celadon. Sung dynasty. Ht. 4·3 in.
Mrs. B. Z. Seligman*

69. *Dish, with carved floral design. Northern celadon. Sung dynasty.*
Diam. 7 $\frac{1}{4}$ in.
Mrs. B. Z. Seligman
See page 43

70. *Saucerdish with carved chrysanthemum design. Northern celadon.*
Diam. 8⅛ in.
Fitzwilliam Museum, Cambridge

71A. *Dish with moulded design of flying apsaras and foliage. Northern celadon. Sung dynasty. Diam. 6·3 in.*
71B. *Saucerdish with incised design, a duck amid waves. Northern celadon. Sung dynasty. Diam.* 6½ *in.*
Mrs. B. Z. Seligman

See page 43

72A. *Foliate bowl. From Chü-lu-hsien. Northern celadon. Sung dynasty.*
Ht. 2½ in. Diam. 4¾ in.
The British Museum
72B. *Ewer of melon shape. Northern celadon. Sung dynasty.*
Ht. 7·5 cm. (3 in.)
Mrs. B. Z. Seligman

73. *Flat dish fixed on spurs. Green Chün. Sung dynasty. Diam.* $7\frac{3}{8}$ *in.*
Mrs. Alfred Clark

74A. *Stem cup with foliate edge. Ying ch'ing ware. Diam. 10·5 cm.*
Ht. 5·3 cm.
Mrs. B. Z. Seligman
74B. *Lotus cup, with carved decoration. Ying ch'ing ware. Sung*
dynasty. Ht. 6 in.
Sir Harry Garner

75. *Vase with incised decoration. Ying ch'ing ware. Sung dynasty.*
Ht. 12⅞ in.
The British Museum
See page 43

76A. *Conical bowl with foliate rim and incised design. Ying-ch'ing ware. Diam. 4·8 in.*
Mrs. B. Z. Seligman
See page 43

76ɪ. *Conical bowl, with incised decoration. Ying ch'ing ware.*
Diam. 5·75 in.
The British Museum
See page 43

77. *Ewer of melon shape with floral decoration, with lion on lid. Ying ch'ing ware Yüan or later. Ht. 5½ in.*
Fitzwilliam Museum, Cambridge

78. *Bowl with combed decoration. Ying-ch'ing ware. Diam. 4·5 in.*
The British Museum
See page 43

79. *Bowl with foliate edge and incised design of dragons and waves.*
Ying-ch'ing ware. Diam. 8½ in.
R. Bruce
See page 43

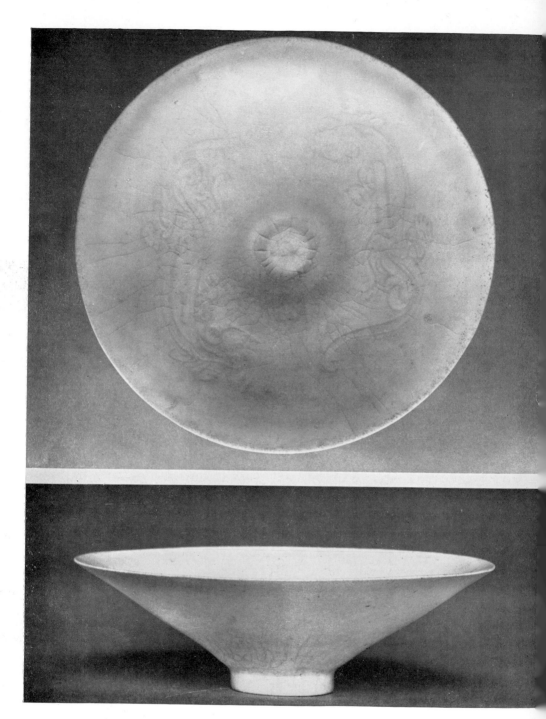

80. *Conical bowl with incised design of dragons and pearls. Ying-ch'ing ware. Diam. 6½ in.*
Mrs. Alfred Clark

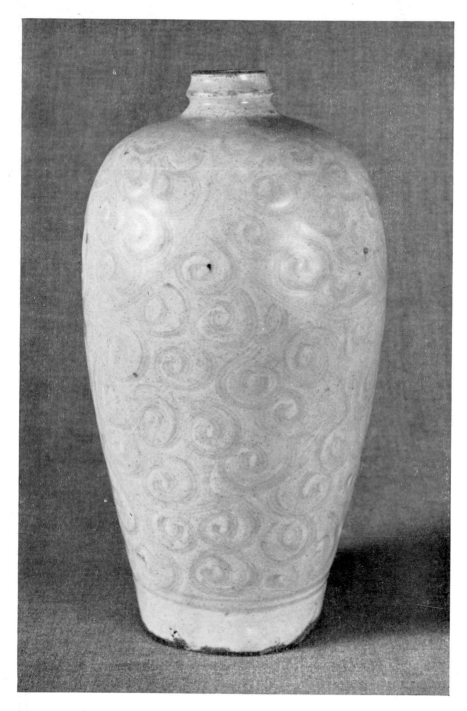

81. *Vase of* mei-p'ing *shape, with incised design. Ying ch'ing ware.*
13th-14th century. Ht. 9·7 *in.*
The British Museum

82A. *Bowl with foliate rim. Chün ware. Sung dynasty. Ht. 2¾ in. ×
Diam. 3½ in. Mrs. Alfred Clark*
82B. *Covered jar. Chün ware. Sung Dynasty. Ht. 3·3 in.
The British Museum*

83. *Two-handled bowl. Green chün. Sung dynasty. Ht.* 4·4 *in.*
The British Museum
See page 32

84. *Dish. Chün ware. Sung. Diam.* $7\frac{3}{8}$ *in.*
Mrs. Alfred Clark
See page 31

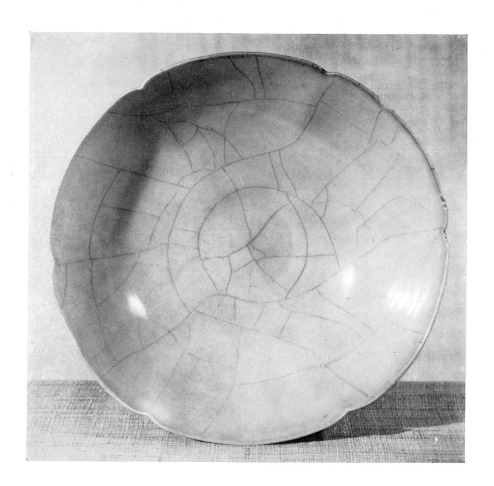

85A. *Bowl. Southern Kuan ware. Sung dynasty. Diam. 7 in.*
Chinese Government
85B. *Saucerdish with foliate rim, showing at the broken edge the dark*
body and thick glaze. Southern Kuan ware. Sung dynasty. Diam. 7·2 in.
Sir Harry Garner
See page 37

86. *Vase with bluish-grey crackled glaze. Southern Kuan-yao. Sung
dynasty. Ht. 5½ in.
Said to be from a grave in Chekiang
Sir Alan Barlow, Bt.
See page 38*

87A. *Brush-washer with foliate edge. Kuan-yao. Sung dynasty.*
Diam. 7 in.
The Percival David Foundation
See page 39
87B. *Incense burner, with dark body and crackled glaze. Ko type.*
Southern Kuan. Sung dynasty. Ht. 6¼ in.
The Percival David Foundation
See page 40

88. *Bowl with lotus design incised under the glaze. Lung-ch'üan celadon.*
Diam. 5·35 in.
Mrs. B. Z. Seligman

89. *Covered jar. Lung-ch'üan celadon. Ht.* $2\frac{7}{8}$ *in.*
The British Museum
See pages 41–42

90. *Vase with phoenix handles. Lung-ch'üan—Kinuta—ware. Ht. 11 in.*
Fitzwilliam Museum, Cambridge
See pages 40–42

91. *Covered vase. Lung-ch'üan celadon. Probably Yüan dynasty.*
Ht. 11 *in.*
R. Bruce
See page 42

92. *Flat dish with narrow rim. (Carnation leaf green.) Lung-ch'üan
celadon. Sung dynasty. Diam. 6¼ in.*
Mrs. Alfred Clark

93. *Ewer. Lung-ch'üan celadon. Probably* 13*th century. Ht.* 10·4 *in.*
The Percival David Foundation
See page 42

94. *Vase with decoration in applied relief. Dated* 1327 A.D. *Ht.* 28·1 *in.*
The Percival David Foundation
See page 42

95. *Bowl, with combed decoration outside and moulded design of phoenixes inside, under a bluish glaze of Shu-fu type. Yüan dynasty. Ht. 3½ in. Diam. 8 in.*
The British Museum
See page 44

96. *Bottle. Crackled green glaze over a light body. Sung dynasty.*
Perhaps Tung-yao. Ht. 8 in.
The Percival David Foundation
See page 36